HAUNTED YORK COUNTY

HAUNTED YORK COUNTY

MYSTERY AND LORE FROM MAINE'S OLDEST TOWNS

ROXIE J. ZWICKER

Published by Haunted America
A Division of The History Press
Charleston, SC 29403
www.historypress.net

Copyright © 2010 by Roxie J. Zwicker
All rights reserved

First published 2010

Manufactured in the United States

ISBN 978.1.60949.101.7

Library of Congress Cataloging-in-Publication Data

Zwicker, Roxie J.
Haunted York County : mystery and lore from Maine's oldest towns / Roxie J. Zwicker.
p. cm.
Includes bibliographical references (p.   ).
ISBN 978-1-60949-101-7
1. Haunted places--Maine--York County. 2. Ghosts--Maine--York County. I. Title.
BF1472.U6Z98 2010
133.109741'95--dc22
2010034173

Notice: The information in this book is true and complete to the best of our knowledge. It is offered without guarantee on the part of the author or The History Press. The author and The History Press disclaim all liability in connection with the use of this book.

All rights reserved. No part of this book may be reproduced or transmitted in any form whatsoever without prior written permission from the publisher except in the case of brief quotations embodied in critical articles and reviews.

Dedicated to those who know that folklore and ghost stories are part of our rich New England history.

CONTENTS

Acknowledgements   9
Introduction   11

GHOSTLY YARNS FROM THE SEA
The Ghosts of Wood Island Lighthouse (Biddeford Pool)   13
The Phantom Ship: The *Isidore* (Kennebunk)   19
Haunted Shipwrecks and Memories (Wells)   24
Last Watch at Goat Island Lighthouse (Kennebunkport)   27
The Lost Souls of Boon Island Lighthouse (York)   28
The Sea Serpent of Wells Bay (Wells Bay)   33
The Bleeding Curse (Biddeford Pool)   34

HAUNTED HOUSES
The Haunted Dream House (Lebanon)   37
Vacationing with the Ghosts (York)   43
The Emerson Wilcox House (York)   46
Jane's Ghosts (Kennebunk)   49
Ghost of the Blue Boy (South Berwick)   51
The Kingsbury House/Waldo Emerson Inn (Kennebunkport)   54
The Ghost of Charles Swett (Kennebunk)   55
A Spirited Welcome at the York Harbor Inn (York)   57

Contents

The Captain Lord Mansion (Kennebunkport)	59
The Kennebunk Inn (Kennebunk)	62

Witchcraft Tales
The Widow's Witchcraft of 1796 (Arundel)	65
The Witches of Sanford (Sanford)	67
The Beaver Dam Witch (Berwick)	69
Witch Grave Mystery (Kennebunk)	70
Betty Booker (Kittery)	72
A Bad Neighbor (York)	74
Witchtrot Road (South Berwick)	75
Mary Nasson (York)	77

Cemetery Stories
The Burial Ground of the Unfortunates (Kennebunk)	83
The Mysterious Burial of Theodore Heard (Wells)	84
Old York Burial Ground (York)	86

Mysteries and Legends
Obe's Ghost Lights (York)	91
Keeping the Peace (Wells)	93
The Haunting of Bryant's Hollow (Shapleigh)	94
Fort McClary (Kittery)	99
Old Gaol/King's Prison (York)	102
Saco River Curse (Saco)	105
The Ghostly Child of Zion's Hill (Kennebunk)	106
The Devil's Invention (York)	107
Hackmatack Playhouse (Berwick)	108
The Hurd Manor/Angel of the Berwicks (North Berwick)	112
The Lost Village of Tatnic Hill (Wells)	116
The Sawtell Murder (Lebanon)	118
Old Trickey the Sandman (York)	122

Bibliography	125
About the Author	127

ACKNOWLEDGEMENTS

A special thank-you goes out to the following people and organizations for their assistance in gathering information for this book: Jack Johnson, Victoria Cook, Pamela Smart, Rustie MacDonald, Mary Lavoie, Jeremy D'Entremont, Michael Guptill, Jane Shapleigh Edgecomb, Friends of Wood Island Lighthouse, the Old York Historical Society, the Brick Store Museum, the York Harbor Inn, the New England Ghost Project, the McArthur Public Library (Biddeford), the D.A. Hurd Library (North Berwick), the Lebanon Maine Historical Society and the Waterboro Public Library.

INTRODUCTION

All we know is still infinitely less than all that remains unknown.
—*William Harvey*

York County, Maine, is a combination of beaches filled with summer visitors and historic homes almost as old as the settlement of New England. There are long, winding dirt roads leading into dark woods where shadows dart from one area to another. Once proud factories now stand silent years after the Industrial Revolution ended. Gravestones in ancient cemeteries crumble away a little more with each passing year.

The landscape of southern Maine is constantly changing, but with those changes come discoveries. New home and highway construction yields forgotten cemeteries and the remains of long-forgotten ancestors. Old factory tunnels echo the footsteps of explorers looking to connect with remnants of the past. Cold drafts and shadows in the mirrors surprise some visitors to old sea captains' mansions on majestic hills.

For many of us native New Englanders, there is no place that we would rather live. We've grown up with ghost stories all around us, and it's almost impossible to escape the tales of the haunted place down the road. So many of these ghost stories cause us to take a closer look at our surroundings and wonder about our history. Haven't you ever peered

Introduction

through the rusty gates of an old cemetery or slowed down as you drove past a spooky-looking house?

It has been my pleasure to peruse old historic archives and to read handwritten and typewritten stories from years ago. Conducting interviews with some of the locals has been a joy, and I hope that collecting these oral legends in this book will help keep them alive. So light an extra candle, lock the door, find a comfortable chair and get ready to take a journey into York County's haunted past.

A dismantled clock tower from the old mills in Biddeford is now a roosting home for pigeons as some of the relics of the city's industrial past slip away.

GHOSTLY YARNS FROM THE SEA

The Ghosts of Wood Island Lighthouse

Biddeford Pool

About two miles east from the mouth of the Saco River is Wood Island. In 1808, the first lighthouse was built on the island, and it was plagued with structural problems for the first twenty years. The coastal weather was harsh on the lighthouse; it wasn't long before it developed leaks and the tower became unstable. The stone tower that currently stands on the island was built in 1839. It has been able to stand up to the harsh winters that Mother Nature orchestrates along the rocky Maine coast. The last Coast Guard lighthouse keepers moved out in 1986, and there were whispers of ghost stories while they lived there. In recent years, the ghosts at Wood Island Lighthouse are not just heard, but they are also seen.

The Coast Guard no longer maintains lighthouse keepers at Wood Island; rather, the beacon is automated and the keeper's house closed up tight. A nonprofit group called the Friends of Wood Island Lighthouse (FOWIL) is responsible for preserving this wonderful historic landmark and educating the public on its history through tours and events. Some volunteers with the group were sharing stories about the unusual goings on at the lighthouse, such as hearing mysterious voices and objects being moved without explanation. The group decided to further delve into the lighthouse's haunted history by inviting a group of paranormal investigators, called the New England Ghost Project, to the lighthouse.

In October 2005, the group from the New England Ghost Project made the journey from the north shore of Massachusetts to Biddeford Pool. The group was made up of Ron Kolek, founder of the group; Maureen Wood, a medium and intuitive; Leo Monfret, a photographer; Karen Mossey an EVP (electronic voice phenomenon) specialist; and "Thermal" Dan Parsons, an infrared camera specialist. After taking the boat ride out to the lighthouse, the group established a home base of equipment in the kitchen. Surveillance cameras were placed in the four bedrooms of the keeper's house and in the lantern room of the lighthouse.

While the group explored the lighthouse tower, a strong ghostly presence was reported. Maureen began feeling the strong energy of a spirit as they climbed the spiral staircase. Once they were inside the lantern room, the presence grew stronger. The spirit that Maureen claimed to have encountered was so strong that she doubled over with chest pain. She described the spirit as cold and clammy, like death, as she grabbed her chest and tried to breathe. The experience was so strong that Ron insisted that the spirit leave Maureen, (sometimes an entity will enter the body of a person and not depart). It is thought that a spirit can feel everything a medium does, including breathing, and that alone can give the spirit a sensation of being alive.

From inside the keeper's house, the folks tending to the equipment relayed that the temperature was dropping quickly, a certain sign that there was ghostly activity. Ron began to question Maureen about the spirit that she was encountering. He wanted to know if it was the spirit of one of the lighthouse keepers. Maureen responded that the spirit had only thought himself to be a keeper, but he really wasn't. Ron then asked if the spirit had died by his own hand, to which Maureen replied, "Yes—a head injury." A couple of questions later, Maureen had trouble breathing again and became unnaturally cold. Ron once again insisted that the spirit leave her alone.

Ghostly Yarns from the Sea

The group reconvened in the kitchen to discuss the events that had unfolded in the tower. During that time, Karen, the EVP specialist, had been listening to her recordings when she said that she picked up a voice saying, "I think the shot got them." The group decided to go to the attic of the keeper's house to see if further evidence could be found. Strange green lights appeared to move around the room, but there wasn't a spirit who wanted to communicate.

After exploring other areas of the property, Maureen had a frightening experience on the long wooden boardwalk that connects the lighthouse to the boathouse. Maureen described seeing dark shadows moving back and forth in front of her. Some of the shadows swooped over her head, and she felt that they were trying to make contact with her by entering her body. All of a sudden, Maureen dropped to the ground and began to crawl, almost as if she were injured. Ron decided to intervene and stop the spirits from entering Maureen and, quite possibly, attacking her.

The night wasn't over yet, as there was still the basement of the house to explore. The entire group of investigators and the volunteers who accompanied the group gathered in the dark basement for what would become the most memorable experience of that October night. Maureen made contact with a male spirit who seemed to express sincere remorse over something. Then a female spirit made her presence known to Maureen. The infrared camera caught an image of a floating orb that transformed into a female form. It glowed with a light from within and, after a minute, vanished.

The group from the New England Ghost Project had no idea how close they had come to the actual history of the island. One of the most notorious events on the island dates back to 1896. The headlines of the *Biddeford Daily Journal* read:

>Shot Another, then Himself
>*Murder and Suicide at Wood Island Yesterday.*
>*Repeating Rifle the Weapon.*
>*Howard Hobbs killed Frederick W. Milliken.*
>*Bullet in his own Brain.*
>*Liquor Mainly Responsible for the Tragedy.*

The story read that a man named Howard Hobbs was "frenzied," and he shot and killed Frederick Milliken at 4:45 p.m. on June 1, 1896. Frederick was thirty-five years old and married. A special officer and game warden, he owned two buildings on the southern end of Wood Island. Howard was about twenty-four years old and lived in one of those rough-looking buildings with another man. Eyewitness accounts told the story that Howard had spent the night before in Old Orchard Beach drinking himself into a tumult with a friend. Deputy Sheriff Duff threatened to throw the two men into jail for the night for drunk and disorderly conduct. The men begged and pleaded not to be thrown in jail, and the sheriff gave them a stern warning and sent them on their way.

The next day, they made their way back out to Wood Island and began drinking again. Officer Fred Milliken attempted to stop Howard so that he could talk to him. Howard seemed intent on something and passed right by Fred without stopping. He went to his house and grabbed his gun—a .42-caliber repeating rifle. He then headed back to talk to Fred, while his roommate, Moses, tried to discourage him from bringing his gun along.

When Fred saw Howard approaching with the gun, he asked if it was loaded. Howard laughed and said that it was not. As Fred continued to walk toward the man with the gun, Howard shot at him, point blank. Fred's wife saw what happened from the nearby porch of their house and rushed to his side. She helped Fred, who was bleeding badly, into the house and placed him on a bed, while Moses went to get the doctor. Howard seemed to have sobered up from the incident, and he tried to help Fred.

Mrs. Milliken asked Howard for the gun, but he told her to stay back or she would get shot too. She pleaded with him to go and see the lighthouse keeper, Orcutt. Howard headed toward the lighthouse and told Orcutt the whole story. The keeper rushed to the dying man's aid, but he arrived just as Fred was passing. Howard declared that he was going to go home and put a bullet through his temple. A short time later, a shot was heard. No one dared to investigate.

When Moses came back from summoning the doctor, he went back to his house and climbed up to the sleeping loft, where he found

Howard—dead. Blood and the rifle lay on the quilt next to him. Embedded in the timber of the house was the bullet; it had gone right through Howard's head, and blood oozed from his temple. Next to him were a goodbye note and a request to deliver a letter to a woman on shore.

The doctor determined that Frederick Milliken died from the bullet that entered his abdomen and lodged in his liver. While there had been no previous altercations between the two men, Howard did apparently owe some rent to Fred. Mrs. Milliken felt that Howard had committed the murder because of the alcohol. She was left with three stepchildren from Fred's previous marriage, and it was noted that she showed deep calm and patience throughout the entire ordeal.

The story of the murder-suicide puts the experiences of the investigators in perspective. However, they decided that the lighthouse needed one more investigation in 2006. The events that led up to that investigation seemed most unusual from the start.

A man in Missouri had a terrifying dream; he felt such fright when he awoke that it seemed real. In the dream he saw a weatherworn shack in a very remote place. Four girls were being held against their will inside, and each was murdered over a period of time. A man's face appeared in the dream over and over again, and two words were repeated: "Wood Island." The man who had the dream was so affected by his vision that he decided to search on the Internet for something by the name of Wood Island. He was able to find a link that mentioned the prior investigation by the New England Ghost Project. When he clicked over to the organization's website, he was shocked to see the face in his dream: that of Ron Kolek.

Taking a chance, the man in Missouri decided to call Ron and explain what had happened in his dream. Ron documented the man's story, put it in an envelope and mailed it to an undisclosed location. He knew that it wasn't going to be long before the group was back at the lighthouse for another investigation. He didn't want Maureen to know the story, so he kept it a secret.

When the date of the investigation arrived, Ron was accompanied by Maureen, Leo and a reporter from the *Biddeford Saco Courier*. There were also other curious folks who joined them that night, including Maureen's husband, the FOWIL historian, Sheri Poftak and a guest. After all of the equipment was set up, the group began its investigation.

While Maureen was dowsing with a pendulum along the boardwalk, she was approached by a female spirit. Maureen said that the lost spirit seemed to need help and that she had been murdered by an Indian on the island. The spirit passed, and the group moved on. They stopped at another location just off the boardwalk, where Maureen attempted to make contact through dowsing once again.

While focused on her dowsing, Maureen revealed that where they were standing was a burial site for more than three girls. The spirit said that the girls were killed in a shack and it was set on fire.

Ron was astonished at hearing this, as it seemed identical to the Missouri man's dream—about which Maureen knew nothing. Maureen went on to say that the people who died were being held against their wishes and that they wanted their story to be told.

The next stop on the investigation was the basement of the house. That was the area where there had been so much activity the last time the group was there. Maureen's sense was that there was a spirit present, but it could not communicate. A ghostly light flashed in the room, and Maureen said that the spirit was angry with them because it had been caught on film last time. They decided to leave the spirit alone and move on elsewhere in the house.

The group decided to revisit the attic; they formed a circle and held hands. The sounds of heavy rain fell on the roof, and almost as quickly as it had begun, it stopped. Other noises were heard, heightening everyone's senses. All of a sudden, Maureen started to speak, but it wasn't her voice. It was the tone of a deep, gruff, male voice with a Spanish accent. He had said that he had been on the island for 360 days in 1762 and that his name was Roger. He claimed to have originally been left on the island with nine other men, but he was only one of three who were left. When asked what flag he flew under, he claimed no flag, to which Ron replied that he must have been a pirate. The spirit took great offense to that statement and told Ron to choose his words carefully.

Maureen began to tense up, and she felt colder and colder as the minutes passed. Ron asked the spirit to leave, and the voice echoed out,

"No!" Inhuman sounds were heard coming from Maureen as her body began to shake. The grip that Roger seemed to have over Maureen was released, and she began to warm up and relax a bit. A wisp of blue smoke swept across the room and dissipated.

The group settled down, and Maureen—who was exhausted—decided that she had had enough for the night. As everyone lay down, all seemed quiet in the house, except to Maureen, who said that she could still hear voices talking throughout parts of the house.

The history of Wood Island Lighthouse (the fifth-oldest lighthouse in Maine) has certainly had its dramatic moments. The island saw daring rescues at sea just off the edge of the island during severe storms and rowdy, brawling Frenchmen who recklessly set fires in the late 1800s. In 1960, the lighthouse keeper's two-year-old daughter, Tammy Burnham, became deathly ill during a raging storm. Coast guardsman Edward Syvinski was thrown out of a rescue boat while holding little Tammy, and he went underwater. He managed to find his way to a nearby island, where they were rescued, and Tammy was brought to a hospital and recovered.

The scenic island with tall sea grass and short, shrubby pines is quite inviting to those who care to have a glimpse of a proud lifestyle of days gone by. The long walkway from the boat dock leads to the weathered keeper's house, while the beacon from the tower sends its light out to sea. Lurking in the shadows and dark corners are ghosts and spirits that move about the property and aren't afraid to reach out to the living.

THE PHANTOM SHIP: THE *ISIDORE*

Kennebunk

Superstitious tales and the sea are closely intertwined in York County. Maritime history is incredibly rich along the coast of Maine, including everything from shipbuilding to fishing and lobstering. For hundreds of years, long before railroads, everything from goods to people moved

The grave marker in Kennebunk for Captain Leander Foss tells of the wreck of the *Isidore*.

by the sea. The sturdy ships that made these voyages were subject to many challenges from sudden, intense weather and the jagged, rockbound coast.

Built in Kennebunkport, the *Isidore* was a sturdy and seaworthy bark that weighed in at about 396 tons. From the very first day that work began on the ship, a strange and unusual air hung over it. It was recalled that the shipbuilders worked in what was described as a gloomy silence. Whistling and light conversation were typically common in boat-building yards as the sounds of hammers and saws resonated in the air, but not around the *Isidore*. It seemed that all shreds of merriment and happiness were stripped from the scene as soon as the *Isidore*'s keel was laid.

November 30, 1842, the day the *Isidore* was launched, was gray and dreary. The sky hung low over the ocean, and the distant horizon appeared shrouded in darkness. The day seemed shadowed from the start. The boat had just started down the ramp to meet the rising tide when it swayed from side to side, and a collective gasp could be heard from the crowd. The lean and slope of the ship led many watchers to believe that it wouldn't even make it to the sea. Despite the apparent concern, the *Isidore* held its own once it was fully afloat in the cold waters of the Kennebunk River. It was then moored to a wharf, ballasted and made ready for its maiden voyage to New Orleans. The north-northeast breeze slowly strengthened throughout the day.

The ship's captain was thirty-six-year-old Leander Foss, who was regarded as one of the best skippers on the Maine coast. The first mate was Clement Stone, and John Crowder was second mate. Both were experienced, dependable mariners. The crew was assembled from some of the best sailors from Kennebunk and Kennebunkport: George P. Davis, William B. Harding, Alvin Huff, George T. Hutchins, George B. Lewis, Charles Lord, James C. Murphy, Daniel H. Perkins, William J. Thompson and James Young. Captain Paul Grant was a local man who joined the company as a passenger. Another sailor, Thomas King, had also signed on to the trip. He had already been paid a month's wages as part of his contract, but he refused to go.

Thomas was a man of unwavering integrity and a dedicated member of the Baptist Church. However, two nights before the *Isidore* was to set sail, he had nightmares about the voyage. He dreamed of a terrifying storm that overcame the ship and proved disastrous for the bark. The vessel was completely destroyed, and all of the sailors drowned. The dream was so realistic that he woke up with his heart pounding. The next night, Thomas had the same exact dream, and the fright he woke up with actually caused him to leap from his bed. Shocked at her husband's behavior two nights in a row, his wife asked him what was wrong. Thomas said that he would not sail on the *Isidore*, to which his wife replied that he would have to since he had already accepted a month's pay. Thomas had made his decision, though, and insisted that he would not go.

The next morning, Thomas went to Captain Foss to return his advance pay and asked to be released from his contract. When Captain Foss heard Thomas's reason for wanting to be discharged from his contract, he refused and dismissed the man's story as nonsense. Thomas sought advice from a friend, who agreed that he should not go. Some say that Thomas hid in the woods on the morning the *Isidore* was to set sail. Wherever he hid, no one saw him over the next few days.

Another sailor also spoke of a nightmare he had the night before the ship was to set sail. In his dream, he described seeing himself standing on the decks of the *Isidore* as it set sail down the Kennebunk River. A strange glowing light enveloped the ship as it sailed over the rolling waves. The next thing he saw were seven coffins floating toward the shore. He asked someone in his dream who those coffins were for, and the voice that answered told him that one of them was for him.

At the home of another sailor, dogs howled for the three nights before the *Isidore* was to set sail. His wife thought it was a bad omen.

Minutes before the *Isidore* cast off, another sailor who had signed on to the voyage ran across the wharf just in time to climb aboard the bark. A friend of his stepped forward to wish him well and told him that he had almost been left behind. The sailor responded that he had wished he were left behind. He scrambled on board and spoke to no one else.

The *Isidore* finally set sail just before noon on that fateful November day. It is remembered that the mood of the crowd that assembled on shore was very dismal and subdued. Cheering and well-wishing was usually heard from the townsfolk, but on this day there was none. The crew was also eerily quiet on the ship as it floated away on the tide. It was said that the loved ones of the crew wept out loud on the shore, many fearing the premonitions that had been mentioned in the recent hours. As the afternoon progressed, the northeast winds began to increase, and a light snow began to fall.

At sunset, the *Isidore* was seen just off Boon Island in nearby York, Maine. The waves began to intensify, with thirty-foot swells, and the snow was becoming blinding. By midnight, the storm had become a screeching gale. The *Isidore* was doomed. One can only imagine the panic and terror of the captain and crew on that fateful night on the tempestuous ocean. In the morning, the tragedy of the night was revealed along Avery's Cove in York, six miles west of Boon Island. The splintered ship washed ashore in pieces; the bow was visible but was covered in water. The ship's cargo of lumber littered the rocky shoreline.

Some people believe Captain Foss may have made the decision to sail back to Kennebunk, but it was too late.

Minister John Pottle was one of the first people at the scene of the wreck in York. He waited with the wives and friends of the crew to see if any bodies washed ashore. Only seven bodies were recovered, including that of Captain Leander Foss and, coincidentally, the mariner who had the dream of the seven coffins. Thomas King, the mariner who had refused to sail, returned a few days after the disaster and learned of the terrible tale. While his family was happy to see him, there were many people in town who were angry at his actions.

About ten years after the wreck of the *Isidore*, tales of a phantom ship were told. Local fishermen along the coast described seeing a ghostly ship sailing along Avery's Cove and out by Boon Island. Some fishermen were afraid to relate their experiences of seeing this ghostly ship because it had disappeared right before their eyes and just didn't seem possible. Sightings of the phantom ship have been seen from Kennebunk, Maine, down to Rye, New Hampshire. It is described as sailing without any sound, with tattered sails and a crew on deck that just seems to stare off into the distance. When approached, it just sails off into the mists and vanishes. Some mariners have reported that they have tried to throw a line to the ship, but it only turns and sails away. It is believed by some that the ship is still sailing, looking for the man who refused to fulfill his obligations to sail on the *Isidore*'s maiden voyage. Others believe that it is a reminder of the perilous dangers of the coast during a storm.

In 1912, the *Maine Sunday Telegram* recounted the story of the *Isidore* and included additional commentary regarding the ghost ship by reporter Chandler Briggs Allen:

> *The yarn of the Phantom Ship may be rejected as a product of superstitions and morbid imagination, it matters nothing. But even the hardest headed person must accept well-substantiated and incontrovertible facts, and there are enough to make one wonder if, after all, there might not be a grain of truth in the yarn the sailors used to tell.*

Haunted Shipwrecks and Memories

Wells

The great artist Vincent van Gogh was quoted as saying, "The fishermen know that the sea is dangerous and the storms terrible, but they have never found these dangers sufficient reason for remaining ashore." This statement certainly rings true in the seaside community of Wells, Maine. The weather can be serene and the beautiful blue of the ocean beckoning, yet that scene can often turn tragic with a sweep of the wind and the surging of the sea. Ocean View Cemetery in Wells is full of sea-soaked fishermen and mariners who lost their lives to ocean tragedies. All one needs to do is stop and read the inscriptions on the gravestones. The Joshua Bradgon monument lists a number of disasters at sea:

> *George—born July 9, 1798, Lost at sea, Feb 1, 1823. Oliver—born Sept. 3, 1802—Died at sea, Feb., 1, 1823. Joseph—born Dec. 1, 1808 Lost at sea, Dec. 31, 1831. Sons of Joshua and Sarah Bragdon.*

Joshua Bragdon's son, Captain Samuel Bragdon, lost two sons as well. Samuel W. was lost at sea on December 30, 1849, at the age of twenty, and John died in the West Indies on April 2, 1866, at the age of thirty-one.

The earliest recorded catastrophe at sea dates back to October 25, 1707, when five fishermen in a small sloop were overtaken by heavy seas. Military ventures and expeditions also claimed many lives in the first one hundred years of settlement in Wells. One of the most unfortunate losses that occurred on Wells Beach relates to Moses Wheelwright and John Eaton. On October 11, 1895, the pair left early in the morning for a fishing trip about fifteen miles out to sea. Conditions worsened throughout the day as a storm blew in and the Atlantic turned violent. The dory that they had taken out was seen struggling with the wind and heavy seas, trying to find its way through the storm to the shore. Search parties were assembled, and groups combed the beaches and held watch for any sign of the pair. Their lunchbox with fresh but waterlogged

Ghostly Yarns from the Sea

Ogunquit, Maine, was originally known as Wells up until 1980. What forgotten shipwrecks lie on the ocean floor just beyond the beautiful beaches?

food washed ashore, along with two oars in two separate places. It was thought that the boat was heavily ballasted and that it may have sunk. Crowds assembled at the church for a memorial, but the bodies were never recovered.

In early July 1915, the ship *Mary E. Pennell* was bound from Perth Amboy, New Jersey, to Lubec, Maine, and it seemed to disappear sometime during an intense storm. Initially, no one knew that the remains of a broken chair and the body of a dog that washed ashore on Drake's Island were related to the ship. It wasn't until almost a month later that much of the wreckage was revealed, along with the gruesome discovery of a decayed body lashed to the ship's cabin door.

Some of these shipwrecks and disasters at sea have yielded a number of ghost stories in Wells. Near the Mile Road Bridge there are still remnants of two fishing schooners, the *Emma S. Osier* and the *William Walker*. A collection of old newspaper clippings reported that the wreck of the *Osier* was actually quite haunted. It was written that on stormy, windswept nights a strange glow appeared over the hulk of the ruined wreck. The story was that a member of the crew had fallen overboard at sea, and despite all efforts, his body was never recovered. His young wife was so overtaken by grief that her heart broke, and she soon followed him to the grave. It was believed that her spirit came back on stormy nights to look for him on the ship where his feet once trod.

A fall storm in 1932 washed away the wreck of the *Robert W.* from Wells Beach. The ship originally had sailed from the busy port of Rockland, Maine. It was said that for the previous twenty years, on September 27 at midnight, a high-pitched song would be heard coming from the schooner's hull. It was believed that the wreck of the *Robert W.* occurred at midnight, and a distraught woman on board the ship cried hysterically. When the sounds died out, it was said that the sea claimed her soul. Believers felt that each year on the anniversary of the wreck her spirit returned to repeat her phantom song as a reminder of the tragedy.

Last Watch at Goat Island Lighthouse

Kennebunkport

A flashing white light at Goat Island Lighthouse along Cape Porpoise both warns of the dangerous rocks that have claimed seagoing vessels over the years and serves as a guide into the busy Kennebunkport Harbor. The name Cape Porpoise came from explorer Captain John Smith, who named the island after the school of porpoises he saw there. The first light station on the island was established in 1833, and the current tower was built in 1859.

From the island, one can catch a view of the Bush estate at Walker's point. In fact, during the presidency of George H.W. Bush, secret service agents lived on Goat Island to keep a protective watch over Walker's Point. The lighthouse was the final Maine beacon automated in 1990, and in 1992, under the Maine Lights Program, the lighthouse became property of the Kennebunkport Conservation Trust.

Dick Curtis was a much-loved keeper of the light and island, and many people believe his spirit may still linger at the lighthouse. Locals tell stories of seeing an apparition in the window of the keeper's house and an unusual fog that envelops the island on perfectly clear days. The foghorn was known to sound off for no reason when it was sunny out. The continual sounds prompted complaints to the Coast Guard. Sensors in the unit were changed, and later the unit was replaced, but it would still sound without explanation. Strangely, even when the power was disconnected, the unit would sound on a regular basis.

It was Memorial Day weekend in 1992 when Dick Curtis went missing. Dinner preparations had been made in the kitchen of the keeper's house, but Dick's boat wasn't moored. It was thought that he was off for a brief jaunt. He had taken his dog with him, along with a few others that he was watching. He seemed to have disappeared, and an extensive search was undertaken. Sadly, late in the second day of the search his body was recovered along the north side of the island in what appeared to have been a boating accident. It was believed that a strong wave upset the boat. It was noticed that the motor on the boat was geared at full throttle in a possible attempt to break free from the current or waves. The community was heartbroken at the passing of a man who always had a smile on his face and a story to tell.

Scott Dombrowski, a lifelong friend of Curtis, has told many stories of his encounters with what he believed to be Dick's spirit. Scott took up the position of keeper and caretaker of the island. The summer following Dick's death seemed to be full of unusual incidents. Visitors to the house saw a vent fan turn itself on without visible assistance. Things that had gone missing would often mysteriously reappear on the kitchen table.

The chill breeze of an afternoon caused Scott to speak out while sitting in Dick's easy chair. He asked his friend for a little heat to warm him; all of a sudden, an electric heater that hadn't worked for years turned on and began to warm the room. Scott had become comfortable with the presence on the island, and he would often greet Dick out loud as he arrived. He believed he always got a response from his dear friend at one particular spot on the island where he heard the foghorn sound just once in response.

It has been fairly quiet over the past few years on Goat Island. Scott misses the interaction he had with Dick's spirit, and he hopes that it won't be long before he'll have a little reminder of his dear friend. The sparkling waters that surround the island reflect the image of the lighthouse and perhaps the memories of Dick Curtis, who truly loved being there.

The Lost Souls of Boon Island Lighthouse

York

Looking at the ledge of rocks and boulders that make up Boon Island, just six miles off the coast of York, Maine, one can't help but wonder how anyone could have survived in this desolate place. There is no vegetation at all, for nothing grows on Boon Island. The cold, heavy surf that washes over the island adds to the sense of desolation, danger and loneliness. The year 1682 is the one on record for the first shipwreck.

The *Increase* was a local ship that made regular runs up and down the coast, but heavy swells tossed the ship onto Boon Island's ledge. Since it was July, the men were able to survive for thirty-one days by catching fish and eating sea gull eggs. When they saw smoke coming from a Native American ceremony on Mount Agamenticus, they salvaged what they could to create a fire on the island. A few days later, the four men were rescued after their smoke was spotted.

On December 11, 1710, the ship the *Nottingham Galley* ran aground on Boon Island during a severe gale. Captained by Jack Dean, the ship had a crew of fourteen men and was sailing with a cargo of ship's rigging, as well as a supply of butter and cheese. Hurricane-force winds battered the ship, and the jagged ledge of the island ripped out the vessel's underside. The crew clambered on to the frozen rocks as the thirty-foot waves destroyed the ship behind them. Temperatures dipped below zero, and the wet clothes the men were wearing hastened the beginning stages of frostbite.

There wasn't much that could be salvaged from the ship except a small amount of butter, cheese and a piece of the canvas mainsail. The sail helped to deflect some of the harsh winter winds, but it was just a few hours into the second day when the ship's cook died. He was buried at sea. The crew was able to salvage a few pieces of wood and constructed a makeshift raft to try to get closer to York Beach, which the men could see off in the distance. However, the raft was blown out to sea, and the two men on it were thrown into the icy Atlantic Ocean, where they drowned.

Although there were a few rough pieces of wood left, there was nothing the men could use to make a fire. The rest of the crew tried to survive by eating raw seaweed and sea gulls, but their stomachs reacted violently. Frostbite set in, and some of the men's extremities began to rot. On January 1, 1711, the ship's carpenter died, and the men were just about out of food. Captain Dean struggled with the notion of keeping the men alive by using the dead body as a food source. The grim decision was made to carve up the body, as the captain felt that there was no other choice. The men held a short funeral service and then quartered the body into pieces; the head, hands and feet were thrown into the ocean.

Some of the men, being God-fearing, refused to take part in this act of cannibalism; however, starving to death didn't seem like an option, either.

Having used the body to survive, the shipwrecked crew was spotted a few days later by a passing ship. The men spent a total of twenty-five terrifying days on Boon Island, and none of them would ever be the same again. The hands and feet of the crew were so affected by frostbite that none could ever use them again after being rescued. The captain was the only survivor who returned to the sea when the ordeal was over.

In June 1995, three five-foot-long cannons believed to be from the *Nottingham Galley* were discovered by divers and archaeologists from the University of Maine and the Maine State Museum. The wreck of the *Nottingham Galley* is one of the most famous shipwrecks on the southern Maine coast, and it is still the subject of articles and stories to this day.

According to a deed on record in 1799, Daniel Weare sold Boon Island to Tom Frost for $1.25. The island was described as "being one and half acre at the low water mark." That was also the same year that the United States government decided that this perilous ledge must be identified, and the day marker on the island was built. Due to a severe storm that destroyed all of the newly constructed buildings, another had to be built in 1805. Three men working on the second stone tower drowned during its construction.

The first lighthouse was built in 1811. The first keeper left his post after just two months because he found the station too isolated. The second keeper only lasted for a few years before he decided that he wanted to turn the command over to someone else. In 1831, a relentless storm destroyed the lighthouse, and a temporary light was constructed from its rubble. Finally, in 1855, a new, stronger tower was completed. Standing 137 feet tall, it is the tallest lighthouse in New England. Made from gray granite rocks that are 5 feet wide and 2 feet high, the stones interlock together, making the tower quite strong. Lined with brick walls inside, there are 167 steps to the top.

There are many legends and ghost stories about the island that have been collected over the years. One of the most fascinating tales concerns a keeper and his young wife who tended to the light station in the nineteenth century. A harsh storm lashed out across the island, sending waves and rocks tumbling from one end to the other. The keeper decided to make sure that his boat was secure, as it was his only way off the island.

His wife watched as he slipped on the wet rocks and hit his head. She ran out to him and brought his body back into the base of the lighthouse, which was only about eight feet around. She managed to climb the 167 steps to the top for the next five days, keeping the light lit and tending to her unconscious husband. When she ran out of fuel for the light, it went out, alerting the passing mariners that something was wrong.

When the fishermen got to the island, they found the woman still sitting in the base of the freezing tower, holding her husband's half-frozen, dead hand. It was said that the woman was hysterical, and she didn't realize that he had died. She was carried off the island, and it's said that she died some weeks later. Many people believe her spirit is still on the island. Later keepers of the lighthouse described hearing a woman's voice speaking in the tower when they thought they were alone. Other encounters with the ghostly spirit include hearing a knock on the door of the keeper's house. When the door is answered, a ghostly woman stands outside and then quickly turns and heads toward the lighthouse, where she disappears.

A storm in November 1945 struck with deadly force, and the waves broke the glass windows in the lighthouse tower. The four people on the island (including three light keepers and one of their wives) barely escaped with their lives, as most of the buildings were leveled to debris. Some of the buildings were eventually rebuilt, only to be destroyed again in the famous blizzard of 1978. The keepers during that harrowing storm clung to the spiral staircase in the tower as the wind and waves battered the island. When they were finally rescued, evidence of the force of the storm could be viewed by looking at the base of the tower. There were scars and indentations where massive boulders had been thrust against the base of the tower.

Solar panels have replaced the waterlogged generators that once powered the lighthouse. In 1986, the remaining rubble from the buildings on the island was burned by the Coast Guard. In fact, more stories have been relayed by the Coast Guard over the years. Coast guardsmen have said that cats and dogs refuse to go in the tower and that, on one occasion, one dog appeared to chase after something invisible on the island. Sounds of someone climbing the spiral staircase have been heard when there is no one else in the tower. Seabirds blown off course often smash into the tower blindly, and sometimes they can be found in knee-deep piles at the base of the lighthouse.

Some of the local mariners describe seeing mysterious fires burning on the island, yet there is no one around and no materials on the island to start them. The apparition of a woman is often seen on the edge of the island where the rounds meet the sea. She is said to have a sad expression on her face as she looks off toward the horizon.

Celia Thaxter, one of New Hampshire's best-known poets of the nineteenth century and daughter of Thomas Leighton, keeper at White Island Lighthouse at the nearby Isles of Shoals, penned a poem called "The Watch of Boon Island." Below is an excerpt:

> *Inexorable Death, a silent guest*
> *At every hearth, before whose footsteps flee*
> *All joys, who rules the earth, and, without rest,*
> *Roams the vast shuddering spaces of the sea;*
> *Death found them; turned his face and passed her by,*
> *But laid a finger on her lover's lips,*
> *And there was silence. Then the storm ran high,*
> *And tossed and troubled sore the distant ships.*
> *Nay. Who shall speak the terrors of the night,*
> *   The speechless sorrow, the supreme despair?*
> *Still like a ghost she trimmed the waning light,*
> *   Dragging her slow weight up the winding stair.*
> *With more than oil the saving lamp she fed,*
> *   While lashed to madness the wild sea she heard;*
> *She kept her awful vigil with the dead,*
> *   And God's sweet pity still she ministered.*
> *O sailors, hailing loud the cheerful beam,*
> *   Piercing so far the tumult of the dark,*
> *A radiant star of hope, you could not dream*
> *   What misery there sat cherishing that spark!*
> *Three times the night, too terrible to bear,*
> *   Descended, shrouded in the storm. At last*

The sun rose clear and still on her despair,
  And all her striving to the winds she cast,
And bowed her head, and let the light die out,
  For the wide sea lay calm as her dead love.
When evening fell, from the far land, in doubt,
  Vainly to find that faithful star men strove.
Sailors and landsmen look, and women's eyes,
  For pity ready, search in vain the night,
And wondering neighbor unto neighbor cries,
"Now what, think you, can ail Boone Island light?"
Out from the coast toward her high tower they sailed;
They found her watching, silent, by her dead,
A shadowy woman, who nor wept nor wailed,
But answered what they spake, till all was said.
They bore the dead and living both away.

THE SEA SERPENT OF WELLS BAY

Wells Bay

On July 21, 1830, a boat filled with three fishermen in Wells Bay was rocked by something that emerged from the deep. The seawater rained down from a large creature that had surfaced to face the terrified men. Two of the men turned fearfully away and quickly hid below deck. Mr. Gooch was the one man who remained on deck to see the fantastic being.

According to a story printed in the *Kennebunk Gazette*, Mr. Gooch was quoted as saying:

> *The serpent was a full 60 feet in length and six feet in circumference, his head about the size of a ten gallon keg, having long flaps or ears, and his eyes about the size of those of an ox, bright and projecting from his head, his skin was dark gray and covered with scales, he had no bunches*

on his back. When he disappeared he made no effort to swim, but sank down apparently without exertion.

It was a little more than five years later, in November 1835, when Captain Peabody of the fishing schooner *Dove* encountered the beast. He tried to get a good look at the creature, and when he got closer, it sank below the water leaving a tremendous wake. The captain judged the sea serpent to be about sixty or seventy feet in length.

The last sighting was on July 22, 1839. The creature was reportedly seen by over a dozen boat crews fishing in Wells Bay. It was reported to be enormous in size, and eyewitness accounts were recorded in the *Kennebunk Gazette*. By all accounts, the men who reported seeing the sea serpent were credible, respected sources, and their stories were never questioned by the locals.

Over 150 years later, the story of the sea serpent resurfaced. Lobstermen from Biddeford Pool had caught a strange skeleton, which some people believed was part of the creature. The remains were preserved by embalming and placed on display. A Biddeford High School teacher remarked that the skeleton resembled that of a shark. Perhaps the creature has moved farther out to sea or no longer exists, but the story remains part of the maritime folklore of Wells Bay.

The Bleeding Curse

Biddeford Pool

According to genealogical records, Thomas Dyer of Biddeford and Elizabeth Melcher of Arundel were married in 1741. There was believed to have been a relation of Elizabeth's who had a very dark side. In some accounts, he was said to have been a pirate, while other tales describe him as a "mooncusser." Mooncussers were scoundrels who would deliberately wreck and plunder passing ships. At night, the mooncussers would ride along the coast on horseback with lanterns, looking out to sea for any ships that might be in distress or close to the coast. They would then plant lanterns on posts to beckon the ships to come closer to shore. The ships would wreck on the rocky coast, and the mooncussers would kill any survivors and steal as much as they could from the remnants of the ship. They usually disappeared before help arrived. The actual name "mooncusser" has a fascinating origin. When the moon was full or partially full, the decoy lanterns wouldn't fool an experienced mariner, so the villains would often shout or "cuss" at the moon.

Coincidentally, Melcher was himself the victim of a shipwreck on the coast, and a rescue boat was sent out to save the men who were tossed into the frigid waters. The small boat filled quickly as the men scrambled out of the ocean. One of the men in the water tried to pull himself into the boat, which was already overloaded. He pleaded to be brought aboard, but Melcher said no because he thought that the added weight would swamp the boat. The man clung to the side of the boat, still refusing to let go when Melcher reached for an axe. The axe was swung, and the man's hands were cut off at the wrists. As the man slipped into the water, he pronounced a curse on Melcher with his dying breath: "You and all of your descendents will bleed to death." The boat rowed away, and the man disappeared below the waves.

The curse seemed to take hold, for Melcher was afflicted soon after with hemophilia, also known as the "bleeding sickness." According to the story, anyone who had Melcher blood during those days died from the bleeding curse. In fact, for years it was said that in Biddeford, when a man was known to be a bleeder, he "must have Melcher blood."

HAUNTED HOUSES

The Haunted Dream House

Lebanon

There are many quiet roads in Maine where one can go for quite some time without seeing another car. Yet there are also places that have become gathering spaces, where people are drawn by some magnetic attraction to make their homes and answer their own personal callings. Imagine traveling down these quiet country roads and finding your dream home, with every detail that you could have hoped for and envisioned. Now, imagine that dream home coming complete with its own mysteries and spirits.

This is the story of Mary and Jerry Lavoie and their dream house in Lebanon, Maine. In 1991, Mary and Jerry decided to move from busy Salem, Massachusetts, to southern Maine. After looking at house after house over a period of several months, their search seemed to come to an end when they found a house in South Berwick, Maine. Having two small children at the time, they were excited about making the move and settling in. However, the purchase of the house in South Berwick was not meant to be. Complications set in, and one thing after another went wrong until the offer on the house fell through. Ready to renew their quest for a house, Mary sat down with a notebook and wrote down a list of specific traits she would like their house to have. The details included everything from the size of the house to the style of the house—preferably historic or historic looking surrounded by stone walls. The description included that the property be surrounded by thriving woods, full of animals and bird life. Jerry wanted a workshop where he could work on carpentry and cabinetmaking. One of the last things added to the list was Mary's hope to have an old-fashioned graveyard on the property. When the list was complete, Mary and Jerry looked ahead to a weekend of house hunting—with list in hand, of course.

It was late Sunday afternoon; the couple had seen many houses but still had not found what they were looking for. It was now down to the last house on the realtor's list. A long dirt road through the woods greeted them. The road looked similar to an old logging road, which still can be found throughout Maine. Alongside the road as they ventured farther into the woods was a long stone wall that served as the property line. At the end of the dirt road was a small circular driveway. As they stepped on to the property, they immediately felt comfortable; it seemed to be a perfect fit. They waited for the listing agent to arrive and decided to take a walk around the house. The house looked like an old New England–style saltbox, although it was only about twenty-five years old at the time. The property comprised ten acres of land, yet it was surrounded by hundreds of acres of woodlands. There was a scenic old farm field on the other side of the stone wall, and there were more stone walls throughout the property.

The details of the grounds were simply perfect. Near the house was a garden surrounded by low rock walls. There was a circular garden in the front yard, and nearby was a granite seat along with an old round, stone grinding wheel. A small shed seemed like the perfect place to turn into a chicken coop. The garage was quite large, and there was plenty of room for a spacious workshop. An office in the garage was another possibility, as there was enough additional space. There was a small pond on the property—another item for the Lavoies to check off their list. They hoped to use the pond to attract wildlife, and it would also be an ideal place to teach their children how to ice skate as they grew older. Even some of the trees were just perfect. A giant pine tree, most likely a couple hundred years old, stood at the edge of the yard near the stone wall.

The excitement of that day in April 1992 is still very vivid for Mary and Jerry. Once the listing agent arrived, they finally stepped into the house, and they knew that it was a perfect match for what they were seeking. In fact, the house reminded them a bit of houses in their hometown of Salem. Places like the House of the Seven Gables and the Witch House came to mind. The house had the charm of a much older historic home, but it had all of the modern-day conveniences. Mary was a little disappointed when she was told that the closest cemetery was a few farm fields over, but there was also one across the street behind the neighbor's house and many others going down Center Road.

Without hesitation the Lavoies went back to the agent's office and immediately placed an offer on the house. They weren't going to take any chances and wait to decide, as they knew that this was the house for them. It wasn't long before the owner of the house accepted their first offer, and then everything moved quickly. As Mary described it, "it seemed surreal." Closing day came fast, and things were going smoothly, but at the closing one of the lawyers raised the question of a cemetery. He wanted to clarify that there wasn't a cemetery on the property. When he spoke up, the owners looked at each other for a moment and then said, "No, there isn't a cemetery." Mary was disappointed because that seemed to be the only thing that was missing.

Once all of the papers had been signed, the Lavoies were ready to settle in to their new home. As soon as they arrived with their things, they made themselves happily at home. Jerry explored the yard to find the perfect tree to build a tree house for their eighteen-month-old and three-year-old. He was drawn to explore the area near the big old pine tree, and he called out to Mary when he made quite a discovery. Mary came out of the house, and when she walked to where her husband was pointing behind the tree, she couldn't believe her eyes. On top of the stone wall were three headstones stacked on top of one another. Mary and Jerry took the stones off the wall and placed them side by side against the tree, where they could take a closer look. The gravestones appeared to be for a mother, father and son from the 1800s.

The headstones read:

Ezekiel Roberts
Died
Nov. 8, 1825
AE 24 years

Edmund Roberts
Died
Sept 9, 1841
AE 69 y 8 m 20 d

Margaret
wife of Edmund
Died
March 17, 1847
AE 73 y 1 m 17 d

Mary and Jerry were quite puzzled about where the actual graves were. There was the possibility that they were buried underneath the tree, but then again, there were so many places on the property where they could have been interred.

The Lavoies left the gravestones against the tree and prepared for their first night in the new house. They had dinner and settled in for the night. As they fell asleep, they heard little creaks and moans in the house, sounds that took a few minutes to get used to. In the middle of the night, Jerry awoke to bright lights in the hallway coming up the stairs. Since the house was set so far back from the street and there were no streetlights in their area, this occurrence didn't make any sense.

The incident with the lights became the first of many unusual occurrences in the house, leading the Lavoies to the conclusion that they were not alone in the house. Doorknobs rattled for no reason when there wasn't anyone at the door. Items would mysteriously fall out of kitchen cabinets. Strange knocking noises occurred on the inside wooden door to the house, which didn't make sense because there was a glass storm door over it and they never heard it open. The longer they lived at the house, the more the Lavoies realized that there was an unseen presence in the house and on the land. Mary said, "We soon found out that we might not be living alone."

One of the most unusual unexplained occurrences happened one night as the whole family was watching television. A small remote control Batman car turned on and started moving backward in the room. Everyone in the room was startled when this happened. The car kept starting and stopping and moving in circles and backward. A search for the remote control ensued; however, the remote was in a different room entirely, one that was empty. The decision was made to take the Batman car and put it in the attic. The batteries were removed from the remote control and it was also placed in the attic, out of sight.

Mary decided to contact the former owners of the house since the unusual occurrences were happening so often. She thought that perhaps they could shed some light on the strange occurrences. When she mentioned the gravestones that Jerry found, the owner was afraid that the Lavoies wanted to move out and give the house back, until Mary described her list for her perfect house and how the only thing on it that was missing was the cemetery.

Mary was told that the husband of the couple found the stones in the rock wall near the old pine tree when he was looking for rocks to build the gardens around the foundation of the house and in the yard. When Mary mentioned that she had leaned the stones up against the big pine tree to have a closer look, they informed her that they had placed them there, too. The owners had decided to move the gravestones after some people who came to see the house when it was for sale got nervous about seeing them. They claimed that the listing agent told them to put the gravestones back behind the tree where they were originally found. Mary also asked about the strange occurrences in the house; she wanted to know if anything odd had happened while the original owners lived there. The wife told her that things happened all the time—unusual lights in the hall, mysterious knocking—but she said they just acknowledged it and went on with their lives because they believed it wasn't anything harmful.

Although the spirits that the Lavoie family were encountering seemed friendly enough, Mary still tried to figure out where the gravestones belonged on the property. She spoke to a neighbor who grew up next door to her property and had played in the woods around the house. He remembered that the bodies were originally buried in the front yard of the house. Still seeking more answers, Mary contacted the Lebanon Historical Society to see if there was any additional information. The historical society was not even aware that there was a graveyard with gravestones on the Lavoies' property. Small family plots are not unusual throughout New England. Beginning in the seventeenth century, right up through the nineteenth century, many small families were actually buried on their own property, and many of these graveyards remain undocumented.

As time went by, two more children blessed the Lavoie family. As it turned out, one of their children began seeing an apparition of a male figure wearing cowboy-type boots, a long dark jacket and a hat. He could only describe him as looking like Abe Lincoln. It was accepted by the family that this "old man" watched over his land, and the family as well, since he appeared so frequently. Then a foreign exchange student came to stay with the family for a month in the summer. She was so frightened when she saw the old man that she hid in the bathroom one night until dawn. The Lavoies explained that he was a guardian spirit just watching over everyone.

There was a fascinating incident that happened one day while Mary was sitting in the dining room and talking on the telephone. She gazed out the window into the adjacent farm field. All of a sudden, she saw a man walking in the field. At first she thought that it was her neighbor looking for stray cows. In the area of the field where the ground dipped low, the old man kept walking straight along his path. It seemed most puzzling because this was the same exact area where the children would go sledding in the winter, where the ground sloped down at a steep angle. The old man's path didn't change, and he appeared to be walking on air.

As the years went by, additions were built on to the existing garage, enlarging Jerry's workshop and creating additional space. Mary decided to follow her own spiritual path, and in 2004 she opened Crescent Moon Herbals, a new age gift shop, in the expanded space. Mary still sees the old man, and each time, she thanks him for walking the land, protecting the family and for making himself known to outsiders all the time. As a daily reminder of the old man's presence, Mary has placed a small, slated stone carved with the letter "R" on her front porch. She found this small stone sometime after the headstones were discovered. The stone is believed to be an additional marker that goes with the headstones, although it was found in a different part of the yard. It was discovered in the rock garden abutting the main house.

Mary and her family have become comfortable with their spirited dream house, and they have grown used to unexplained encounters. What once may have surprised or startled them is now a welcome experience to connect with the guardian spirit that keeps watch over the family.

Vacationing with the Ghosts

York

What seems better on a hot summer day than to plan a vacation to the cool coast of Maine? Lighthouses, lobster and sea breezes, along with beautiful sandy beaches, invite those who want to get away from it all to York, Maine. York Beach has been a tourist destination since the late nineteenth century. Today, instead of grand Victorian summer homes, most vacationers look for hotels and motels, but for those are who are looking for accommodations like home, there are plenty to be found. There are literally hundreds of weekly rental properties, from beach cottages to modern town houses.

When I was told the following story by a local real estate broker, I promised not to reveal the property's location. There is a popular town house that is busy all summer long with vacationing families. Fully furnished and contemporary, this comfortable vacation rental also comes with a very friendly spirit. There are so many stories about this particular property that there are several real estate agents with their own stories about it. One of the most often told stories relates to a young couple with an infant child about four or five months old. The couple had settled into their town house rental and had gotten ready for a wonderful week of sightseeing, local dining and relaxing. The first night they were in the town house, they heard the sounds of someone walking around on the first floor. They went to investigate but found nothing and no one there. A little uneasy, they went back to bed and finally found some rest.

The next morning, they left the town house and went about their day, seeing the sights as they got their vacation started. When they came back that evening to change and go to dinner, they noticed something that they did not expect when they walked into their bedroom. A clean stack of sheets and pillowcases were placed at the edge of the bed. This seemed rather odd, as the couple had only been there one night, and they didn't think that there was a need to change the sheets so immediately. They contacted the real estate agent by phone to see if perhaps someone had come by and dropped them off. The couple was told that no one had stopped by the town house while the couple was out, let alone dropped off sheets. Even though the couple thought this rather strange, they placed the sheets and pillowcases inside one of the closets and forgot about them as they made their way to dinner.

Later that night, the couple returned to the town house and were preparing for bed when they heard mysterious footsteps on the first floor. They stood at the top of the stairs and listened to be completely sure of what they had heard. The shuffling sounds were unmistakable. Then, all of a sudden, they heard the movement of books being re-shelved on the bookcase in the downstairs living room. They could literally hear the books sliding off the shelf and then being put back into place. They peeked down the stairway, expecting to see someone there, but as they made their way down the stairs, they saw nothing. An extensive search of the town house also revealed nothing, much to the couple's frustration. As they discussed what they had just experienced, their attention turned to their baby, who was laughing in an adjacent room. They walked in and looked into the crib. They noticed that the baby's eyes were fixated on something—or someone. They looked to see what the baby was laughing at, and the baby turned his head to watch with amusement whatever had gotten his attention. The nervous parents picked the baby up and noticed that the child still seemed distracted. He kept turning his head as if looking for someone in the room. Shaken, the couple decided to call the agent to tell him they wanted to be moved to another town house. Quickly, they packed their belongings and left the town house.

One of the agents mentioned that he had heard so many stories about the town house that he decided he was going to stay there and see if they were true. He brought along his girlfriend. He said that he had a hard time sleeping that first night, sensing that there was another presence in the room. However, the noise from the living room was certain: it sounded like someone was walking around and taking books off the bookshelf. He resigned himself to go to sleep, still feeling a bit skeptical about the whole story. There couldn't be such a thing as ghosts—could there?

The next day in the kitchen, his suspicions were finally confirmed. In the morning, as he looked out the window of the town house, he felt an open hand on the back of his neck. He quickly turned, expecting to see his girlfriend standing behind him, but she was still upstairs asleep. He looked around the room; he was alone, but once again he felt the presence of someone else in the room. He checked the front door, and it was locked. He went upstairs and checked on his girlfriend, and she was still fast asleep. He sat on the edge of the bed and tried to figure out what had happened. He went over the unusual things he had experienced in the past twenty-four hours. When his girlfriend woke up, he described what he had witnessed and that he had come to the conclusion that the ghost stories he had heard about the town house were indeed very true.

The town house is still a weekly rental in season, and the stories about it flow into the real estate office every so often. Perhaps the spirit that inhabits the town house is just making sure that guests are comfortable and well taken care of. But for those guests who would prefer to enjoy their vacation with just family, perhaps they might be a little more comfortable in another town house or a nice beach cottage.

The Emerson Wilcox House

York

Originally constructed in 1742, the Emerson Wilcox House in York, Maine, is a wonderful example of Colonial architecture common in the eighteenth century throughout New England. In 1760, the house was doubled in size with the addition of an older building attached to the back of the house. The expansion of the house created a tavern room, and it also enlarged some of the existing rooms in the house. A kitchen and buttery (a small room for storing foods or wines) were soon added. Finally, in 1800, the house had another addition put on that contained a post office and servant's chambers.

The house was originally owned by Abel Whitney and the Reverend Samuel Moody. When Edward Emerson purchased it, he did not officially

According to one man, the Emerson Wilcox House is the most haunted house in York Village.

purchase the land it was built on; rather, there was a 999-year lease on the land that required payment of sixteen ($1.44) shillings annually, expiring in the year 2765. Edward had eight brothers and was originally from Malden, Massachusetts. One of his brothers was the Reverend William of Concord, Massachusetts, grandfather of the poet Ralph Waldo Emerson. Edward had eleven children. Hannah, who was born in 1752, died during infancy.

Part of Edward's house also served as a general store and tailor's shop. The store was filled with a variety of goods, including molasses, brandy, gin, cotton, Dutch linen, brown earthenware, biscuits, Bibles, hardware and women's shoes. According to documents from the eighteenth century, there were "a great variety of English and West India goods, cheap for cash or Treasurer's Notes."

In the 1780s, Edward's eldest son, William, ran a tavern out of one of the rooms in the home. Edward's wife, Mary, became very sick, and she died in 1793. Edward married a second time, but his new wife, Susanna Perkins, died in 1799. He followed her in 1806, passing at the age of seventy-eight. They are buried in the Old York Burying Ground, just behind the house. Edward's daughters Lucy and Ruth were given life rights to live in the house. His son Bulkeley inherited the house, but he died bankrupt in 1815. After Bulkeley's death, ownership of the property was sold to David Wilcox. Lucy, Ruth and Bulkeley's widow all lived in the house, although it was said that it wasn't an amicable arrangement.

The tavern continued to serve mostly as a stagecoach stop until 1828. The tavern room of the building contains a sign listing a timetable for the Boston–Portland stagecoach. Many notable people visited the tavern over the years, from General Henry Knox to presidents John Quincy Adams and James Monroe and the Marquis de Lafayette. David Wilcox was quite involved with the community, having taken several positions, including customs inspector, deputy sheriff and coroner. In 1819, David also served as a delegate to the Maine statehood committee. There were six children in the family, and Louisa Caroline Putnam inherited the house upon her father's death in 1856. The house passed through a few more owners until it was purchased by the Old Gaol Museum in 1953.

Fifty years later, an article appeared in the *Portsmouth Herald* about the house, but it wasn't covering the house's interesting history. Instead, it detailed some of the ghostly encounters that had been experienced there.

Dana W. Moulton III was caretaker of the Old York Historical Society's historic buildings, and he believed that the Emerson Wilcox House was the most haunted of the collection. In an interview, he spoke of hearing loud, mysterious footsteps in the house, feeling cold rushes and finding doors open when they should have been closed. He talked about a particular incident in 1987, when he was just four months on the job, that made him a believer.

Part of Dana's job included checking the building alarms, and one night at 2:30 a.m. the alarm sounded at the Elizabeth Perkins House. Everything appeared to be in order, so after securing the house he began to make his way home. Along the way, he had to make a quick stop at the bathroom at the Emerson Wilcox House, which used to be the visitors' center. He disarmed the alarm and went inside to use the facilities. While in the restroom, he heard a door down the hall open with a squeak, followed by footsteps coming closer. Dana composed himself and fled to the courtyard, where he looked back up at the house and saw nothing. He could not leave without rearming the alarm, so he reached back into the door. He said it was like putting his hand into a freezer; it was ice cold inside. He managed to get the alarm turned back on and left as quickly as he could. Dana said that a dog he once owned often became spooked on the property as well. The dog would bark at nothing and would scratch on the ground like something was there.

The Emerson Wilcox House is open for tours from June through October through the Old York Historical Society. There have even been stories from visitors to the house who have encountered something unusual. A little girl and her mother were taking a tour of the house, and during their visit, the little girl kept pointing to someone—or something—in each room, saying, "I see you." The little girl was asked what it was she had seen, and she mentioned seeing a lady dressed in a white wedding gown whom no one else had seen. A husband and wife were on tour in the house one day when the wife went up the stairs and the husband stayed behind. At the top of the stairs, the wife turned to ask her husband what the delay was. He stated that there was a woman in white standing on the stairs. A little girl on another tour waved at an empty room, and when she was asked whom she was waving to, she said "Joanna." It was believed that Joanna would often make herself known only to children.

The house was also rumored to have moods. In the summer months, when it was open for tours, it was a happy place to be; in the winter, it was described as having a sad atmosphere, almost as if it knew there wasn't going to be anyone around for months. Even some of the York police officers find the building quite eerie; some of them have described hearing disembodied voices coming from the house in the middle of the night when there is no one around.

Many people believe that the house isn't haunted and that perhaps these are just tales of superstitious folks. However, there seem to be quite a lot of ghostly rumors about the Emerson Wilcox House—almost too many to ignore. Should you ever find yourself in Old York Village, it might be worth paying the old house a visit to decide for yourself about the building's spirited past.

Jane's Ghosts

Kennebunk

The historic colonial house on River Road in Kennebunk was said to have been built sometime after 1754 by Gideon Merrill. After being passed down through the family, the house was sold to Samuel Lewis in 1830. Samuel was an undertaker who built coffins with glass tops. His son, George B. Lewis, died at sea—a victim of the wreck of the *Isidore*. The house was owned by several families, and in 1937 it was purchased by Robert Currier. He renovated the barn and spruced up the property over the next three years. On July 2, 1840, the Kennebunkport Playhouse was opened in the newly revamped barn and boasted three hundred seats.

Robert's younger sister, Jane Morgan, known as "Flossie" when she was little, was convinced that the playhouse and farmhouse were both haunted. An internationally known singer and television star, Jane had performed for five United States presidents. She was convinced that there were two restless ghosts roaming the property. There was an intimidating uniformed solider and a sweet woman who wore a long gray dress with a wide white collar.

Eyewitnesses seemed to confirm Jane's experiences, and one woman claimed to have seen the two apparitions in the attic window of the house when there was no one home. The woman became known as Quaker Nellie, and she would often appear for just a few minutes and then vanish. Robert was fascinated by the ghosts, and he invited a psychic to the house to confirm the presence of spirits. Fascinated by the psychic's confirmation, he decided to have a Ouija board session to try and contact the spirits.

One dark night, a small group gathered, ready to connect with the mysterious spirits. According to the story, they got their answers. During the session, it was communicated to Robert's cook that Quaker Nellie liked Robert, but she couldn't be at peace until the actors left the premises permanently. The ghostly activity seemed to increase after the session with the Ouija board. Jane's good friend Muriel Pierce described being woken from a sound sleep by someone in her room. She explained that she saw a Quaker woman surrounded by a gray mist float past the foot of the bed and out the door.

A local newspaper reporter and photographer decided to visit the house in the 1960s, escorted by Jane, who proceeded to show the reporter every corner of the haunted house. She mentioned on the tour of the upstairs rooms that she would securely latch her bedroom door but would often find it unlocked in the morning. One particular incident she spoke of related to a troupe of actors staying in an adjacent room. They were plagued by one of their doors, which continually became unlatched throughout the night. They decided to nail the door shut and went back to bed. Loud crashes and bangs could be heard on the other side of the door, and noise came from the attic. The series of theater performances that followed after that unusual night were plagued with problems. Lighting wouldn't work properly, and the set pieces were moving on their own. This continued until someone decided to go into the farmhouse and remove the nails from the door.

Jane also told the reporter that she believed the soldier (whom she nicknamed "Ned") killed Quaker Nellie because she wouldn't return his affections. Nellie's father, seeking revenge, reportedly killed the soldier, and their spirits were bound to the property. While proof of that incident was never uncovered, Jane felt strongly that their spirits had haunted the house for over one hundred years. The full-page article was eventually printed in the newspaper. The headline read: "Night Brings Naught, Jane's Ghosts Snub Newsmen."

One night after a playhouse performance, Robert was wandering around in the basement of the building. While he marveled at the brick archways that provided support for the building, he found an antique coffin. He pulled it out and opened it but found nothing inside. In 1971, arson claimed the playhouse, and it burned to the ground. The fire was believed to have been set as a diversion by thieves in the area. There are many in Kennebunkport who still have fond memories of the theater and all of the interesting characters that passed through it.

Ghost of the Blue Boy

South Berwick

The town of South Berwick, Maine, was officially settled in 1631, and there are still parts of the town where the woods are thick and the roads are very quiet. Old Fields Road located just off of Route 236 is part historic time capsule, with a wonderful old wooden mill building and many eighteenth-century homes. The name Old Fields Road came from the fact that the land was once used by Native Americans. The Newichawannock Indians used to summer throughout the area long before white men set foot on nearby shores.

The two-story house located at 211 Old Fields Road stands next to a peaceful river that winds through a grove of tall pine trees. A young couple with an eight-year-old daughter rented the house for a few years. One particular night, the couple put their daughter to bed and decided

A simple-looking house along a peaceful road is a regular haunt of the blue boy ghost.

to sit up a while to watch some television. As the house quieted down, the couple relaxed in the first-floor living room. All of a sudden, screams from their daughter's room prompted the couple to run upstairs and check on her. They opened the door to the room and saw her sitting up in bed with her eyes fixed on the window. When asked what was wrong, she said she heard a banging on her window and saw a little boy with a blue face looking back at her. The spirit appeared to be a boy of about

Haunted Houses

Just around the corner from the house haunted by the blue boy is the Old Fields Burial Ground. This ancient cemetery may hold the identity of the ghostly little child who wanders looking for food.

five or six years wearing dark clothes with a cold-looking blue face. The apparition was saying, "I'm hungry" as he tapped on the window. The father turned to his daughter, who was sitting speechless on the bed. He quickly walked over and put his arms around his daughter to comfort her. He knew it had to be a ghost; the bedroom was on the second floor, and it would have been impossible for someone to stand outside the window. They had never known their daughter to have imaginary playmates, and she seemed so certain of what she had seen. They sat up with the girl for a while, but she wasn't able to fall back asleep. It was decided that she would sleep downstairs with her parents.

The couple spent most of that night trying to figure out who the spirit could have been, but they just couldn't seem to figure it out. The family lived in the house for another year, but they often felt a presence in the house that made them think they weren't alone. The blue boy never reappeared.

The Kingsbury House/Waldo Emerson Inn

Kennebunkport

The oldest house in Kennebunkport was originally built in 1753 by Waldo Emerson (the great uncle of poet Ralph Waldo Emerson). Once known as the Kingsbury House, the building held quite a fascination for Betty Joyce, a reporter for the *York Country Coast Star*. On November 11, 1970, Betty published a story about the curious ghostly history of the house. The house was believed to have been haunted by Theodore Lyman, who built an addition to the house in 1780 for his father-in-law, Waldo.

After the passing of Waldo, his daughter, Sarah Emerson, became the sole beneficiary of his estate. At the age of twenty-three, an ambitious Theodore married fourteen-and-a-half-year-old Sarah. During the next few years, Theodore was quite successful in adding to his wealth through ventures in the West India and China trades. Sarah had two children; however, one died at eight days old, and the other died just under two years old. Sarah herself passed away at the age of twenty-one.

Alone, Theodore turned his attention to the empty house. Improvements and updates were completed, and it was considered a fine house for the wealthiest of noblemen. Two years later, after a visit to Salem, Massachusetts, Theodore brought home a new bride from an aristocratic family. While Theodore continued to attend to his thriving business, his new wife was feeling rather forlorn. After four years of marriage, Theodore and his second wife left Kennebunkport forever and moved to Waltham, Massachusetts. When Theodore passed away at the age of eighty-six, he had a larger home than the one in Kennebunkport, and his fortune was very substantial.

The Kennebunkport house passed through several generations of the Kingsbury family. In 1939, a caretaker of the house said that the house was quite haunted, and he claimed to have known men who would not spend one night in the house. Stories of unusual occurrences in the house began to spread, mostly having to do with the closet underneath the stairs. It was said that the closet door would unlatch itself and that mysterious footsteps could be heard ascending the staircase. A little while after the initial noises stopped, it was said that the sounds of someone climbing down the stairs could be heard, and then the closet door would close and lock.

One of the rumors about the house was that the ghostly activity became too much for one of the owners, who called a minister in to bless the house. The activity subsided for a few years. Today, the house has become a comfortable inn, and according to the latest owners, the ghost is no more. A weakened house beam was blamed for the strange sounds; it was said that when the beam was walked over, the door underneath the stairs would pop open. The troublesome beam has since been replaced.

The Ghost of Charles Swett

Kennebunk

In 1793, Abial Kelly purchased land from Dimon Hubbard to build his house. The construction was completed fairly quickly, and in 1794 Abial moved in. About fifty years later, the house was sold to Dr. Charles M. Swett, a newcomer to the area. Dr. Swett had once been a Baptist minister, but he decided to pursue a career in medicine instead. It was rumored that he couldn't have remained a minister because he was much too fond of alcohol. The doctor didn't have many friends and was often seen getting into loud arguments with his neighbors. His medical practice began to dwindle. Jane, his wife, never seemed happy. She often fought with her husband, and he usually got the better of her physically. The problems in their relationship were complicated by the fact that four of their five children died very young.

Jane was also aware that her husband was having an affair, and one day she decided she was done with his drunken brawls. At dawn one morning, Jane sent her fourteen-year-old adopted daughter to the barn to search for the doctor's hidden bottle of whiskey. When the girl returned with the whiskey, Jane uncorked the bottle and poured in forty grams of morphine. She tightly corked the bottle and sent the girl back to the barn to put it back where she had found it.

Later that morning, Dr. Swett went out to the barn and pulled his bottle of whiskey out of the hay where it was hidden. The doctor took a healthy swig out of the bottle and instantly became sick. He stumbled back into the house and collapsed on the couch. When Jane saw his grave condition, she grabbed the bottle of morphine and ingested such a large dose that she vomited it back up. Help arrived for the doctor, but even with the aid of a stomach pump, it was too late. The doctor died at 12:15 p.m.

An autopsy was scheduled for the same day as the trial of Jane Swett: September 25. The stomach was removed from the victim's body and sent to Portland for analysis; it was determined that the morphine had caused his death. A handful of people showed up for the doctor's funeral. The trial continued for some time. Jane admitted to putting the morphine in her husband's whiskey, but she said that she only wanted him to get sick. One February 12 of the following year, the jury convicted Jane Swett of manslaughter. Jane's motion for a new trial was denied, and she was sentenced to the state prison for six years, a term that some felt was too short.

Jane was a very vocal prisoner and made demands that other prisoners wouldn't have dared make. She refused to scrub and repair the inmates' clothes, a duty that she was assigned on a regular basis. Not used to doing hard work, Jane stated that she needed her hands for painting, as she was a landscape artist. Apparently, she caused such upheaval in the jail that she was allowed to go home and retrieve some of her home furnishings, although she did share her cell with a horse thief and a murderer who had been sentenced to hang. When Jane's sentence was through, she returned to Kennebunk and endured hard labor at the town poor farm, where, after several years, she died.

Henry Sargent, a carriage painter, moved into the house and lived a solitary life for over fifty years. As Henry's health declined, so did the condition of the house. The timeworn look on both seemed to show that the end was near. Relatives of Henry decided that he could no longer live alone, and they chose to put him in a home. The night before he was to leave, he took a walk out to the barn, looked at the house one last time and hanged himself.

The house was then sold to Mariette and John DeAngelis, who saw the potential in the property and decided to restore it. They even brought in local antiques that they thought were befitting the house. During the restoration, hidden aspects of the house were revealed behind years of wallpaper and boards. It was discovered that the house didn't have just one fireplace; it had eight. There was a secret small opening behind the chimney where children could climb through and hide in a secret room during Indian attacks. A stone cistern underneath a trapdoor in the kitchen was also revealed when work on the floors began. A forgotten smoke room was also discovered at the back of the house, and it still had the old hooks that would have been used to hang meats on.

Curtains in the house were known to move when there was no breeze, floorboards would creak when the rooms were empty and a voice was even heard coming from the secret room behind the chimney. Is it just the moans and groans of an old house that has finally been able to rest peacefully, or are the ghosts of the past still wandering the rooms of a place they once called home?

A Spirited Welcome at the York Harbor Inn

York

Heading from York Village as you round the corner toward York Beach, you'll find the beautiful York Harbor Inn. The colorful gardens in front of the inn create a picture-postcard view of the lovely structure, but be sure to look across the street from this high point to the ocean vista. It's no wonder that there is a No Vacancy sign hanging out front of the inn throughout most of the summer season. Those who come to stay for a long weekend or a weeklong escape probably don't realize that they are being welcomed by a ghost.

Mrs. Colligan owned the inn from the 1940s to 1979 (back then it was known as the Hillcroft Inn), and she was always known for keeping a careful eye on guests, making sure that they were comfortable and had everything that they needed. Room 12 (the L.L. Bean Room), located at the top of the small staircase above the Cabin Room, was Mrs.

Colligan's personal bedroom. A circular window was cut into the door so that she could look out on guests and employees to make sure that all was well. Although she passed away some years ago, living a happy life into her nineties, her spirit has chosen to remain at the inn, a place she loved dearly.

Many people passing through the inn have described feeling the sensation that they were being watched by someone they couldn't see. There is a rocking chair that rocks on its own. The reflection of a person passing through the room has been seen in the mirrors when no one was passing by. Very early one morning, two employees were sitting in the Cabin Room when they were startled by loud phantom footsteps echoing past them.

The night auditor has even had a few mysterious experiences that could not be explained. Part of the night auditor's duties is to make sure that the upstairs ballroom is locked and secure at the end of the night. In the morning, he would find lights on in the bathroom and the bathroom doors open. Sometimes the night auditor would leave the bathroom door open to see if anything happened overnight, and when he came back in the morning, the door would be closed. All of the activity in the ballroom seems most unusual, because once the door is closed and locked for the night, no one goes up there.

In 2008, the dining room was closed for painting for about a month. White sheets were hung to keep the dust to a minimum. One day, a woman who had an appointment with the wedding planner was walking through the dining room when she saw the shadow of a woman on the other side of a hanging sheet. The visitor reached out and moved the sheet aside, and there was no one there. Heading back to the front desk, she met the wedding planner and described her experience. That's when she learned about the ghost.

A couple getting ready to check out of Room 12 asked a staff member to have their picture taken on the porch outside of the room. The staff member went outside and stood at ground level while the couple posed. Once they were finished, they turned around to head back into their room for their luggage but found the door locked and bolted from the inside. They shouted to the hotel staffer that they were locked out on the porch. Someone went up with a key into the room and unlocked the porch door, much to the delight of the startled but giddy guests.

One chilly evening, one of the staff members was bent over, placing another log in the fireplace of the Cabin Room, when all of a sudden he felt someone bump up against him pretty hard. He looked up and saw what appeared to be a man dressed in a Revolutionary War uniform passing by the mirror. Even housekeepers have heard footsteps going back and forth in the halls when no one is around.

The interior architecture of the inn is very unique, and of course that may be the attraction for many spirited encounters. The Cabin Room structure was originally built in 1637 and was used as a sail loft for the refitting of ships' sails. It was moved to the inn by barge and reassembled. The Ship's Cellar Pub was once a stable for horses, and both were converted into a functioning inn and tavern in 1871.

At the registration desk is a brass pineapple that holds matches. Pineapples are symbolic of hospitality; the belief goes back to the eighteenth century. The top of the pineapple has been known to fly off and land on the floor without reason. It's also gone missing and has turned up in unusual places. New England ship captains would return from long journeys and put a pineapple at people's houses as a symbol of a safe return. Today, the pineapple is a universal symbol that one is welcome to come in.

The folks at the York Harbor Inn believe that visitors and guests should feel comfortable around these harmless spirits, as they are overseers of a place they truly love.

The Captain Lord Mansion

Kennebunkport

Construction on the breathtaking Captain Lord Mansion began during the War of 1812 and was commissioned by wealthy shipbuilder Nathaniel Lord and his wife, Phoebe. Commerce along the New England coast

The Lincoln Room at the Captain Lord House is said to be the domain of a friendly female spirit.

was disrupted by the British blockading the harbors, so Nathaniel put his shipbuilders to work on the house. Fine architect Thomas Eaton designed the Federalist-style home. The mansion was completed in 1814, but unfortunately Nathaniel died in 1815 at the age of thirty-nine. The house stayed in the family for the next seven generations, through 1972. For the next six years, the house served as a boardinghouse for seniors with a few rooms rented to transients.

In 1978, the property was purchased by Bev Davis and Rick Litchfield, and they were excited by the idea of converting it into an elegant and romantic retreat. They went about furnishing the mansion with period antiques, and they named the rooms after ships that sailed in Captain Lord's fleet, such as Harvest and Oriental. The rooms are luxurious, and the inn quickly earned the distinction of being one of the most romantic inns in America. Over the years, many notable people have stayed at the inn, including Paul Newman, Joanne Woodward, Vanessa Williams and David Soul.

One particular room is reported to have a ghostly guest. The Lincoln Room was once known as the Wisteria Room ("wisteria" means "remembrance of the dead"), and it is believed to be inhabited by the spirit of Captain Lord's young wife, Phoebe. Her spirit has been seen floating through the room wearing a white nightgown. On one occasion, she surprised a couple on their honeymoon. Her ghostly form has also been seen on the spiral staircase leading toward the cupola of the house. She has also been thought to be the one who mysteriously closes doors in the house when no one is around.

The mansion stands tall at the top of the village green hill and overlooks the Kennebunkport Harbor with a wonderful view of the current-day maritime traffic. Perhaps Phoebe keeps a protective watch from the Lincoln Room, overseeing the comfort of the guests at the inn. As guests in the room fall asleep on the tall four-poster bed, perhaps they'll catch a glimpse of the kindly spirit floating by in her white nightgown.

The Kennebunk Inn

Kennebunk

Built in 1799, the Kennebunk Inn was built right on Main Street, and with its welcoming front porch, you might be tempted to stop by for a visit. The property was once the private home of Phineas Cole. After passing through several families, George Baitler purchased the building and converted it into a hotel that became known as "the Tavern." An additional two-and-a-half-story wing was constructed, bringing the room count up to fifty. The name of the hotel was changed to the Kennebunk Inn in the late 1930s. By 1978, the inn had fallen into severe disrepair, and it took new owners Arthur and Angela LeBlanc two years to restore the building. It was during this time that the resident ghost decided to make himself known on a regular basis.

The Kennebunk Inn offers delicious food and drink—along with a few ghost stories.

Haunted Houses

One of the waitresses who worked at the inn talked about sensing a presence in the basement, and she was certain that she was not alone when she was down there. She mentioned that the name "Cyrus" came to her, and that's what she decided to call the spirit. It wasn't long before the waitress refused to go to certain areas of the basement because she was constantly picking up on the presence of Cyrus.

The encounters with Cyrus began to happen quite frequently, with much of the staff relaying their own experiences to the owners. One waitress said that she saw a piece of crystal levitate in the air and then crash to the floor. There were a few guests who backed up the waitress's story. A bartender said that he was actually assaulted by the ghost one evening. He said that he was hit in the side of the head by a German mug that normally was stacked on the shelf behind him. The force with which the bartender was hit left a bump on his head, and he felt that the mug had been deliberately thrown at him.

Two of the rooms in the inn also seemed to be favorite spots for Cyrus to visit, as he would often lock and unlock the doors to the rooms. One night, a guest in room number seven said that the door to his room kept unlocking and opening all night long, no matter how many times he got up and locked it. The guest decided that he wasn't going to stay up all night locking the door, so he just left it open all night. Other guests reported feeling ice-cold breezes pass through them in the rooms, almost as if someone they couldn't see was passing by.

As the years passed, it was believed that the spirit Cyrus was actually Silas Perkins, a night clerk at the inn who died sometime in the 1950s. He lived in a room directly above the basement of the inn. He was a fascinating character who once ran a coal business in town and later became a published poet, having works printed in Boston and Portland newspapers. He enjoyed writing so much that he didn't want visitors to stay too long when he worked in the coal office. He sawed off an inch or so of the front legs of the guest chairs so that visitors would be uncomfortable after a time and he could get back to his writing.

The inn was sold in 2003 to new owners Brian O'Hea and Shanna Horner O'Hea. There are now twenty-five guest rooms throughout the inn, and the current owners delight their visitors with incredible gourmet meals. They have been featured on national television with some of their tasty creations. The inn still retains its charm and mystique, with its beautiful and ornate stained-glass windows and a Brasserie-style restaurant where comfort foods are served with a modern twist. Be sure to keep an eye on your wineglass should you visit, as you never know when spirited Silas might stop in and give it a little nudge off the table.

WITCHCRAFT TALES

The Widow's Witchcraft of 1796

Arundel

Originally settled as Cape Porpoise, the pretty town of Arundel, Maine, has gone through some name changes over the years. It was Arundel from 1719 to 1821, then it was changed to Kennebunkport from 1821 to 1915 and then from 1915 it was North Kennebunkport until 1957, when the name was changed back to Arundel. Once a summer grounds for Native Americans, the village developed in the milling industry, including sawmills, a cotton mill and a gristmill.

A different notion of spinning "yarns" seemed to develop in 1796, when a group of local women stirred up a witchcraft controversy in Arundel. This well-documented case can be found in court records of the times, and one can only wonder, if this story had happened in 1692, during the time of the Salem Witch Trials, would the outcome have been the same?

The women involved were Sarah Hilton, Molly Hilton and Dolly Smith, and they accused Widow Elizabeth Smith of witchcraft. The events of October 15, 1796, were recounted in the court records. According to the reports, Elizabeth Smith had incensed her neighbors and relations to such a degree that she was forced to "fly" to a neighboring town for safety. John Hilton said that he was walking home one evening just before dark when Elizabeth appeared before him about six yards away. The ox goad (a pointed spear used to move and prod animals) that he was holding did something very unusual. He claimed that the sharp tip pushed through his hand, moving under its own power, and completely passed through it. He believed that Elizabeth was using witchcraft to make the goad move on its own. In response, John said that he attempted to strike her and instead received a violent blow to his lower back, one that left him reeling in pain.

Further testimony in court by witnesses and John Hilton detailed another encounter with Elizabeth. Days after the incident with the ox goad, Elizabeth had been summoned to John's house in a much more rational manner, and she proposed an antidote to his injury. She declared that John should shed her blood so that he would be "cured." However, a far different version of the story was told by Elizabeth in court.

Elizabeth said that Dolly, Molly and Sarah threatened her and told her that she "ought to have been long ago in hell with the damned." They also told Elizabeth that they would let John loose to exact his revenge on her. Fearful, Elizabeth ran back to her home, and it wasn't too long before John was at her door accompanied by the three women. He dragged Elizabeth out of the house and beat her violently with a stick; all the while, the women shouted, "Kill her, Uncle John. Kill her!" John continued to beat Elizabeth and choked her until she was almost unconscious. That wasn't the only assault on Elizabeth. According to records, other "projects" and "means" were undertaken by the women to put an end to the old woman's life.

The court case was heard in nearby Biddeford and attracted reporters and lawyers from as far away as Boston. At the time of the trial, the court received word that a house near Elizabeth's had been completely vandalized and destroyed. The actions were thought to be a warning to Elizabeth. The judge sitting on the case wasn't about to accept excuses for the deplorable actions committed by Elizabeth's attackers. The women were ordered to pay court fees, and they were told to "keep the Peace and be of good behavior towards all the good citizens…more especially toward Elizabeth Smith."

The Biddeford town history books commend the action of the court and, specifically, Judge Rishworth Jordan and Squire Benjamin Hooper. The history books also point out that this was a case of "sadly, uneducated, superstitious women of Arundel"; however, a judgment of "sanity and intelligence" was reached.

The Witches of Sanford

Sanford

Sanford was officially settled in 1739 and has grown to become the most populated town in York County. One may be surprised to hear that there are stories and legends of witchcraft in the town's early history. One tale concerns a woman simply referred to as "Granny," who was considered by many to be a witch. An incident that occurred in the late 1700s was documented in the town's history books. Elder Richardson was baptizing Granny's son, John, in the nearby river when Granny came rushing down the hill toward the scene and caused quite a commotion. She was dressed all in white and plunged herself into the water. She came up with a shilling and placed it in the hand of Elder Richardson. Instead of grasping the coin, he let it slip out of his hand and drop into the river as he continued with the baptism. Granny then leapt from the water and swept up the hill, almost as if the wind was at her back. Many of those in attendance believed that Granny was possessed by an evil spirit that was trying to stop the baptism. Later that day, as the people walked home past Granny's house, they saw her white clothes hanging on the clothesline, still soaked with the river water.

Granny had a confrontation with a man named Ezra Thompson one day when he was over at his mother's house. One of the visitors at the house looked out the window and saw Granny coming down the road toward the house. Mrs. Thompson said that she didn't want Granny to come in the house because she was afraid of her. Erza stepped to the door to make sure that it was locked, and just at that time, Granny pounded on the door, insisting to be let in. Ezra refused, respecting his mother's wishes. Granny began to shout that if he did not open the door she was going to set a curse upon Mrs. Thompson. Ezra opened the door, closed it quickly behind him and stood on the front step of the house. Granny tried to struggle past him, demanding and shouting that she would go in no matter what. Ezra blocked the door, and despite Granny's attempt to get into the house, he proved to be a strong obstacle. Frustrated, Granny claimed that she was going to curse Mrs. Thompson from where she stood. According to the story Granny began to twist and contort her body as she pronounced her curse. She was described as being as flexible as a snake while speaking. She left in a rush after uttering her final words, while those inside the house covered their ears so as not to hear Granny's vile words.

However, not all stories about Granny were frightening. One day, she was walking along the cornfield when she saw Martha Thompson's grandson, John, working. She asked him what he was doing and how his family was. She then blessed him and the crops he was harvesting.

When Granny died, it was discovered that she had one very curious possession referred to as a witch bridle. The witch bridle was described as being a rope with very curious knots and items tied to it. In some interpretations, this bridle was known as a witch's ladder. Witches ladders originated in Europe during the seventeenth century, and some people believed that they were used for making cow's milk dry up or even for causing people's deaths. However, the witch's ladder was a device used for protective and good luck spells.

Another woman believed to be practicing witchcraft lived in the village of Springvale and was simply referred to as "Old Mother York." The description of her physical attributes was scary enough. She was described as being an ill-favored old hag with no teeth and a beard. Old Mother York was blamed for every misfortune that plagued the town. She was reported to have caused terrible storms, and some people believed that she was even responsible for stillborn children. Some of the claims seemed quite outrageous; she was even blamed for poor-tasting meals.

One story in particular concerned shape-shifting. The tale goes that a man was walking along the road one evening near open fields when all of a sudden a hog ran right into his path. He couldn't seem to drive it away, and it kept running around his feet, preventing him from venturing any farther. The man grabbed some stones and branches on the ground and threw them at the troublesome hog. He struck the beast several times. After many strong blows, the rather bruised hog ran off across the field. The next day, people who encountered Old Mother York remarked on how bruised she was and noted that her head was swathed in bandages. Those who had heard of the evening encounter with the hog believed that the witch had transformed herself into a hog to be a nuisance to the man.

The house that Old Mother York lived in, once owned by Peleg Sanford, was also reported to be haunted. Tales of mysterious sounds and eerie lights flashing in the window were some of the most common legends. It was even said that a traveling peddler was murdered by three people on the property. One of the ghosts in the house was believed to have been Old Mother York, and she was supposedly accompanied by the spirits of the three murderers who were never found.

While the tale of these two witches and their escapades seem a little far-fetched, there were many in Sanford who believed that they were being plagued by these women and their alarming spells.

The Beaver Dam Witch

Berwick

Encompassing twenty acres and located in Berwick, Maine, the Beaver Dam Pond is a scenic spot surrounded by tall trees. The water is quite shallow at only about five feet deep, but it is rather warm and is spring fed. There aren't a lot of fish, and the water can seem quite dark, despite the fact that it is shallow.

Old Marea was known as the Beaver Dam Witch back in the eighteenth century. Described as a troublesome character, she was always causing some form of mischief in town. Her name came from the fact that she lived on the Beaver Dam Pond, in what was portrayed as an old hovel near the road said to resemble a large sand bank. Her abode certainly caused people to wonder how anyone could live like that.

When simple things went wrong, Old Marea was blamed. Something as basic as the butter not churning in a timely manner put people in an uproar, and they believed that she was up to her tricks. In order to discover the evil spirit and overcome it, family members would lay a file across the butter churn and then read a chapter aloud from the Bible. The curse would be broken, and they believed the witch was always revealed by the broken leg she would suffer as a result of reversing the spell.

Today, there's a popular campground along Beaver Dam Lake. The old hovel has disappeared, and the superstitious tales of Old Marea have slipped away. For those in town who still churn butter the old-fashioned way, you may now rest easy and not fret over a witch's curse.

Witch Grave Mystery

Kennebunk

A dusty file labeled "witchcraft stories" can be found at the Brick Store Museum in Kennebunk, Maine. The first paper inside the file will quickly grab your attention. It's an undated letter from Virginia Langley to the editor of Carol Publishing in New York City. The letter begins:

> *Dear Kevin, My forgotten Great, Great, Great Aunt was a witch. That's what the jury said in the mid-1700s. She was hanged! I visited the amazing witch's grave in our town…a solitary grave sealed off from the main cemetery…bear[ing] a leering Devil's head.*

The letter goes on to state that Virginia discovered pages in her family's diary to confirm the story, and she said that she found more information from additional records kept at the historical society. She was hoping to reconstruct the story in the proposed book. By all accounts, the intended book was not published. The mission of the book was quite noble:

> *It can lead today's readers into their own discoveries and adventures among the treasures and documents they find in attics across America. They too may discover witches and pirates among the bones of their ancestors.*

While this all may seem rather enticing, there are some aspects to this story that beg further investigation.

In Kennebunk's historical records, there is no mention of a witch being hanged in the eighteenth century, or at any other time in the town's history. There is the legend of the witch's grave, but the story was, in fact, nothing more than a myth. Reportedly, unusual ceremonies took place around the grave on the darkest of nights. This stone marker with unusual faces bore no inscription or epitaph, so it truly was anyone's guess as to the name of the person buried there.

It was revealed in recent years that the grave marker didn't have a devil's head; rather, it was a protective gargoyle designed to ward of evil spirits. This indicates that the grave marker was not an eighteenth-century carving but a nineteenth-century design. The individual was known to a few in town, and she wasn't a witch; the person was afflicted with mental illness or some form of mental retardation. This individual was alive during the nineteenth century, a time when mental illness was not completely understood and those who were afflicted carried some sort of stigma throughout their lives. Because there was no adequate medical treatment for these people, speculation and rumors were often whispered behind their backs, often making them outcasts.

It would seem plausible that once this person was deceased, the stone was not carved with a name so as not to draw any unwanted attention to the final resting place or the family. Rather, a symbolic stone was placed over the grave instead. Sadly, the grave site located on Sea Road was vandalized after 1994, when the unique marker was stolen off of the grave. More of a mystery, in current times, is the reason the marker was stolen. A public appeal was made and an investigation ensued; however, the stone has never been found.

Betty Booker

Kittery

The legend of Old Betty Booker of Kittery is one that was a favorite told in front of blazing hearth fires and handed down for generations. A fisherman known as Skipper Perkins was known to be a disagreeable old salt. One day, as he prepared to go fishing, the skipper was standing on the Kittery town docks when he was approached by Old Betty Booker. She asked the fisherman to bring her a "bit o' halibut" when he returned. He asked her for a sixpence in response. With a twisted scowl, she asked again for a "bit o' halibut," raising her voice. The fisherman turned and walked away, and it was said that she made a grasping motion in the air behind him. She was described as having a wicked head, wild gray hair, the nose of a hawk and eyes like a snake.

The old Congregational Church Cemetery and the eighteenth-century Lady Pepperell Mansion. Did Betty Booker really frighten Skipper into giving her a load of fish by riding him through town like a horse?

The fisherman sailed off into the morning sun, and Old Betty remained on the docks. Once out at sea, what had seemed like a calm day quickly turned to disaster for Skipper Perkins. Phantom winds tore at his sails and ripped long gashes into them. The waters around the schooner rolled wildly, almost causing it to overturn. His crew became sick and was of no help. Each time the nets were pulled from the water, there wasn't a single fish in them. After an exhausting day, Skipper returned to port, a bit worse off than when he had departed that morning.

Some of the men in town told the fisherman that they had heard Old Betty Booker was going to make a witch bridle for Skipper. They said that it was her intent to throw the bridle over Skipper and ride him like a horse through the streets of Kittery. The fisherman arrived home early that night. He double barred his doors, blew out the candles and sat in the dark, terrified of what was going to happen next. The door to his house shook late that night, and he heard Old Betty's voice bellowing that she was going to come back for him when the next storm came.

The next morning, Skipper Perkins was not seen on the docks. Neither was Old Betty; however, black clouds could be seen moving closer on the horizon. A storm was coming. Within hours, driving rain in blinding sheets moved across Chauncey's Creek. The wind ripped through the trees, and branches could be heard cracking and snapping as night fell quickly. There wasn't a soul to be found anywhere in town; everyone had holed up in their houses. Some whispered that the witches were out.

That night, Skipper not only double barred the door but he also moved some furniture up against it. He braced himself, as he knew that it wouldn't be long before Old Betty showed up. All of a sudden, at the height of the storm, the front door to the Skipper's house began to shake, and there was a loud scratching on the wood. The raspy voice of Old Betty could be heard. She kept asking for "a bit o' halibut" over and over again. Skipper pushed against the furniture, hoping to brace the door closed, but it shook wildly. A screech echoed form the other side of the door, and then it suddenly flew open. The pouring rain blew into Skipper's house. He leapt onto the bed and wrapped himself in the covers.

Old Betty was accompanied by two other witches, who quickly jumped on Skipper and tore at his clothes. Old Betty wrapped her bridle around

Skipper and climbed on his back. The fisherman was helpless and felt more like a horse than a human as Old Betty lashed and kicked him. They disappeared out the door and into the stormy night.

A couple weeks went by, and Skipper Perkins had not been seen. Although the door was back on his house, there was no answer. Early one morning, as the fishermen gathered at the town docks, Skipper appeared, displaying bruises around his neck. Without a word, he climbed into his schooner, assisted by his crew, and sailed off to fish. He was the first fisherman to return that day, before sunset. Old Betty Booker was standing on the docks with a smug look on her face. The first load of halibut was brought up and presented to Old Betty for her to make her selection. She took several fish, turned and walked away without paying a dime for them. When she was gone, Skipper Perkins told the other fishermen about that stormy night.

Years later, an old house in Kittery was being torn down, and an old witch bridle was found between the boards in the wall. It was described as being made from the tail of a horse and strands of tow; the inside was the bark of a yellow birch tree. A woman who was present when the bridle was discovered realized what it was, and she quickly threw it in a fire.

A Bad Neighbor

York

In March 1758, the deacon of the First Congregational Church in York made a startling announcement:

> A strange distemper has seized upon my sheep by which thirty, old and young, have died apparently bleeding at the nose. Soon after all the hens and chickens were found dead with their necks twisted. A fine calf was bright and well in the evening, in the morning he was found on his back with his legs up panting until he died.

He went on to describe other unusual incidents that took place in his house: Kitchen utensils that had been carefully placed turned up in the fire, partially burnt, after he turned his back for only a moment. He said that his children were all eating porridge one day and the spoons were taken right out of their hands and went missing. A visitor over for coffee was warned not to put her spoon down or it would disappear. The woman laughed and placed the spoon inside the coffeepot and closed the lid. A few minutes later she checked on the pot and the spoon was gone. Other strange things were happening as well, causing the family a bit of distress.

It was thought that fasting and a good dose of prayer would settle things. Many parishioners became quite concerned for Reverend Lyman. Finally, the strange happenings were blamed on the influence of witchcraft—on a bad neighbor whom the deacon had offended. The daughter of the neighbor who knew of the rumors about her father implored him to stop his "disturbing enchantments." From that point on, all was quiet in the Reverend Lyman household.

Witchtrot Road

South Berwick

Witchtrot Road is a long road that connects to Route 91 and meanders along quiet spaces in South Berwick. There are many old homesteads along the road that hearken back to the road's earlier days. But the name of the road is most curious itself.

Reverend George Burroughs was once the minister in Salem, Massachusetts, during the time of the Witchcraft Trials. Abagail Williams accused the reverend of practicing witchcraft and called him the "Black Minister." The minister and those faithful to him left Salem and traveled to Wells, Maine. He had hoped to be as far away from the madness in Salem as he could get. Reverend Burroughs was held in high regard by the residents of Wells; they saw him as an Indian fighter and a hero. The reverend had led a successful defense of the village garrison during

There are many historic homes that stand along Witchtrot Road in South Berwick, Maine. Many visitors believe the infamous road is haunted.

a recent Indian attack. He began to minister once again. However, on April 30, 1692, an arrest warrant was issued to bring him back to Salem to stand trial.

The magistrate burst into the reverend's home in Wells and quickly took him out to be brought back to Salem. The minister was quite certain that he could prove his innocence and agreed to go peacefully. He even suggested a timesaving shortcut through the backwoods.

The men took the shortcut the reverend spoke of, but as the four men rode horseback in an isolated area of South Berwick, a severe lightning storm blew in. Blue flashes of lightning flared across the road, and the trees bent wildly in the heavy winds. The sky grew black and ominous, and of the four men, the reverend was the only one who was not afraid. The men from Salem believed that the minister had conjured the storm through his use of witchcraft. As the group continued up and down the hills of the road, the tree branches bent down and reached out like possessed arms. The path they took is now known as Witchtrot Road.

Once back in Salem, the men testified that the reverend had cast a spell on them and had called the four horsemen of the apocalypse to come down on them. The minister denied any wrongdoing, but he was sentenced to death for being a witch. From the gallows, the reverend recited the Lord's Prayer perfectly, without missing a beat, a feat that was thought to be impossible for servants of the devil. Cotton Mather, who was present at the hanging, insisted that the execution proceed that day in August 1692.

Superstitious folks who travel Witchtrot Road believe that it is haunted, and there have been stories of cars stalling or getting mysterious flat tires. Those who dare to walk the road at night have described seeing visions of specters hiding in the trees watching them. All of these ghost stories, however, have not stopped many people from building their homes on the legendary road.

Mary Nasson

York

One of the most popular legends in York, Maine, is that of Mary Nasson, whom some believe was a witch. She was just twenty-nine years old when she died in 1774, and within one hundred years of her burial, local history books referred to her as a the "Witch of York Village." It was believed that Mary was an herbalist, and for those who were seeking healing cures, Mary always seemed to know what was needed. She stocked quite a cabinet of herbs (not an uncommon practice in the day) and, according to some accounts, was eager to help those in need. Mary was also visited by some because they believed that she could dispel bad spirits. Some legends say that in order for women to be unafraid of ghosts or spirits, they have to be practicing witchcraft. How else would they have knowledge of the spirit world? Could it have been that Mary was braver and more knowledgeable than most women? No one knows for certain, as the story of Mary has been passed down through so many generations.

One thing for certain was that a legend grew up around Mary's burial site in the Old York Burial Ground. Her remarkable gravestone is a portrait-style stone carved by the Lamson family of stone carvers from

The legend of the witch's grave tells that the long stone slab was placed over the body of Mary Nasson to keep her from rising up out of the grave. However, in reality, it is a wolf stone designed to keep the animals from digging up the body.

Witchcraft Tales

Mary Nasson's striking headstone was carved by the Lamson family of stone carvers in Boston, Massachusetts.

Boston, Massachusetts, and it was commissioned by her husband Samuel. The image on the stone depicts a woman with large eyes, coiffed hair with a shroud around her shoulders. The inscription on the stone reads:

> *Here liest quite free from Lifes*
> *Distressing Care,*
> *A loving Wife,*
> *A tender Parent dear*
> *Cut down in amidst of days*
> *As you may see*
> *But—stop—my Grief*
> *To Soon shall equal be*
> *When death shall stop my breath.*
> *And end my Time*
> *God grant my Dust*

*May mingle, then, with thine.
Sacred to the memory of Mrs.
Mary Nasson. wife of Mr. Samuel
Nasson who departed this life
Augst. 28th 1774
Æt. 29*

    Although Samuel had hoped to be buried with her, it is believed that he was laid to rest in the family plot in Sanford, Maine. Mary's grave site once had an angelic footstone; however, it was damaged in recent years during upkeep of the burial ground. There is a long stone slab that lies on the ground that many have called the witch's stone. The rumor was that it was placed over Mary's body to keep her from rising up out of her grave. The truth of the matter is that the stone is called a wolf stone, and it was placed over her grave to keep the animals from rooting up her body. Wolf stones were fairly common throughout New England, and some can still be found in older towns in Connecticut.

    It was recorded in one of York's history books that during the eighteenth century, folks leaving Sabbath services noticed hogs digging around the fresh burial plots. Also, an old map of the burial ground drawn by an elder in the community showed that there were many graves that had wolf stones. All of the wolf stones, except for Mary's, had gone missing over the years. One theory was that they were used to raise up the stone wall around the cemetery. Some stones could have been taken to build other stone walls or for use as part of foundations for houses. Every few years, a story will turn up in Maine's newspapers about old stone steps to homes that, when turned over, are discovered to be gravestones. Perhaps some of the stones became steps to some of the houses in town.

    Another theory that lends itself to the witchcraft legend was that if a visitor to Mary's grave touched the stone on the ground and then touched the headstone, he would find that the stone on the ground would be much warmer because Mary's power was emanating from the grave. Truly, there is a scientific explanation for the temperature change. There is a large opening in the trees in the area of Mary's grave where the sun shines through all day long and warms the stone on the ground.

Witchcraft Tales

According to an old book about York called *The Ancient City of Gorgeanna, Modern Town of York*, Mary Nasson couldn't have been a witch for the following reasons:

> *She died too young…she had been married, and witches never or seldom marry. A gravestone would not have been permitted for her in the burial yard. If [she was] a witch, she would have been interred in the rough sands of the sea, at low water mark, with the tide ebbs and flows twice in twenty four hours, or on a highway at the junction of three roads.*

Despite the facts, the legend of Mary Nasson lives on, and there are some who think that she is a ghost. Paranormal groups from all over New England have been drawn to Mary's grave to investigate the ghostly possibilities. Some investigators believe that they have captured EVPs of disembodied voices at Mary's grave. Others believe that they may have caught a glimpse of her on film.

There was also a legend that a playground that was once directly across the street from Mary's grave was haunted by her. Children reportedly were being pushed on the swings by someone they couldn't see. Hand-tied bunches of wildflowers would be left in the playground and around Mary's grave, almost like an invitation to visit. According to the Old York Historical Society, there are no records of a playground across for Mary's grave. That space is now being used as a parking area for visitors to the Old York Historical Society.

Visitors to Mary's grave are left to ponder the mystery of Mary's life and to decide for themselves if she was a witch or if the legend grew up around the grave. Those curious about the spirit world may always be drawn to the grave site because of the ghost stories. One thing is for sure: the tale of Mary Nasson is one of the most fascinating legends of York Village.

CEMETERY STORIES

The Burial Ground of the Unfortunates

Kennebunk

Hidden in the woods on the west side of the Kennebunk River is an unmarked burial ground with approximately thirty graves. This was a place where the "unfortunates" were laid to rest. Many of these people lived out their days in the local poorhouse, surviving on the kindness of others. It was said that the greatest treat for many of those people would have been a carriage ride through the countryside. Some locals believed that their despondency turned them into people with mental problems, as it was thought that being destitute somehow erased memory.

The shocking and rather sad tale of one man who was laid to rest there is the most legendary story of the burial ground. This man, who died in 1863, was born into a prosperous family in Kennebunkport. Lured by the sea, he felt that the ocean was his calling. He started working on ships as a cook and rose through the ranks as an able-bodied crew member. He served a term in the United States Navy, and when it was over, he was still in love with the sea. He took a position on a merchant ship. On one of the ship's voyages, it encountered a hurricane at sea and wrecked on the island of Barbados.

He found his way on to a British ship bound for London, England, and along the way, he was impressed into His Majesty's navy. Armed with a pair of pistols and a cutlass, he did quite a bit of fighting in the short time he was enlisted. During one exchange, the sword of an enemy blinded him in one eye and disfigured him for life. When he learned that America was at war with Britain, he refused to fight and wanted to go home. The British government, however, sentenced him to Dartmoor Prison, which was used to hold prisoners from the War of 1812. Eventually, his record was reviewed, and the British government freed him. He was penniless, and his spirit was completely broken by this time. He applied to the American consul for passage home. When he returned home and arrived on his mother's doorstep, it was said that she refused to believe he was her son. He was bearded, scarred and sick and looked much older than his years. Over the following years, he could no longer find work, and his frightening appearance kept many people away from him. Seeking refuge and help in the poor house, it's said that Kennebunk was the only town that would take him on as a burden.

Today, this unfortunate man sleeps forever in the unmarked graves deep in the woods a short distance from where the town farm used to be. His incredible story and true identity was laid to rest with him under the shadows of the trees.

The Mysterious Burial of Theodore Heard

Wells

An odd story comes from Wells, Maine, and relates to the unusual burial of a man named Theodore Heard. To find this strange tomb where he is interred, follow Route 109, Sanford Road, to a little mound of dirt set back from the road. The tomb is covered with granite slabs leaning against one another. The front of the tomb is also covered in granite; however, dirt and native plants conceal most of it. There is a barely legible marble tablet that reads: "The Family Tomb of Daniel Heard, Sept. 1815."

It was believed that Theodore was one of eight children born between 1767 and 1788 to Daniel and Lydia Heard of Wells. Lydia died in 1812, and it is believed that Daniel had the tomb constructed after her death. Daniel, who was a sea captain turned farmer, passed away in 1822 and was also buried in the tomb. Daniel's son, Theodore, was simply known as "Thed," and he was confined to a wheelchair for most of his life. One of his dying wishes was to be buried sitting up in his wheelchair, and some believe that this is one of the reasons the tomb was constructed.

During the 1950s, a local historian decided to delve into the story he had heard of the "man buried in his wheelchair." He interviewed many people, and while there were some who had heard of the story, many details were missing. Finally, following a tip he received, he met local man, Austin Goodwin, who confirmed that he had heard the story of the wheelchair. He said that the chair was wheeled with the body sitting upright into the Heard tomb. There was no coffin or burial shroud.

Following another lead, the historian was able to connect with taxi driver Clinton Morrison, who seemed to know everything about everyone. Clinton agreed to drive him out to the mysterious tomb. Along the way, he mentioned that he had been driving a cab along Sanford Road for years and always cast a wary eye at the tomb from across the road. Clinton recalled that as a boy he was frightened by seeing the specter of Thed's ghost rolling right out of the front of the tomb, almost as if he were coming directly toward him.

After conducting personal interviews and piecing the story together, the historian documented the tale as best he could. It was published in the *Boston Globe* and was entitled, "The Man Buried Sitting Up." This story has been lost to dusty archives, but one must wonder, does the spirit of Thed still roll out in his ghostly wheelchair and get a view of the modern world passing by?

Old York Burial Ground

York

One of the oldest existing burial grounds in Maine was established around the year 1700. The original burying place for the first settlers of York was a small burial yard full of simple fieldstone markers. Around the 1950s, the burial ground was overturned to build summer cottages, and the remains of the settlers were buried underneath the foundations of new houses.

Located across the street from the Congregational church and the town hall, the burying ground stands like an ancient museum full of images of skulls and cherubs, accompanied by some of the more famous names in the town's early history. The oldest stone dates back to 1705, and the newest stones are from the mid- to late 1800s, when the burial ground stopped being used.

Within the burial ground are a variety of fascinating stones, including a memorial to the victims of the 1692 Indian massacre. The Abenaki Indians attacked the village on Monday, January 25, 1692, a religious holiday known to the English as Candlemas Day. Madockawando, the Abenaki chief, led 150 warriors, and at sunrise they swept into the village. The Reverend Shubael Dummer tried to flee on his horse, but he was shot. The murder of a minister caused particular fright for years to come. Cotton Mather expressed his thoughts about the murder in his writings: "Those bloodhounds…had long been wishing they might embrue their hands in the blood of some New England minister and in this action they had their diabolical satisfaction." It was reported that one of the Indians stripped the minister of his clerical robes and paraded before the captive villagers, taunting and frightening them.

The massacre went on for several hours as houses were looted and then burned, villagers were taken captive and many victims were scalped. Some of the captives were marched to Canada, while children and young girls were often ransomed. It took some time for the village to recover and rebuild. Over the years, there were other attacks, but none was as devastating as the 1692 attack. A large memorial stone placed by the Society for the Preservation of Historic Landmarks marks what is believed to be the mass grave for approximately forty of the victims of the 1692 massacre. There are no names on the tablet, which is located at the front and center of the burial ground.

Some of the epitaphs in the burial ground reflect the religious sentiments of the early villagers:

John Bragdon
a promising Youth,
departed this life
June 19th, 1744.
in ye 23d Year of
his Age; with
some comfortable
Hope in his Death
after great Distress
of Soul & solemn
Warnings to young
People, not to put
off the Repentance
to a Death Bed.

In Memory
Of
Jonathan Sayward, Esq.
Amiable and social in address,
instructive and entertaining in conversa-
tion, benevolent, charitable and pious,
uniting the gentleman and christian.
Various offices, Civil, Judicial and
Ecclesiastical with honour & reputation
he sustain'd
he died May 8, 1797
Æt. 84.

Some of the graves display both a footstone and a headstone. The use of two stones was typical in the seventeenth and eighteenth centuries. The headstone served as symbolic of the headboard of a bed and the footstone was symbolic of the footboard of a bed, with the body lying in between in eternal sleep. Some of the footstones appear to be almost completely out of the ground, while some headstones have sunk so far into the ground that it's difficult to read the entire inscription on the stone.

The 1785 gravestone for Ruth Lyman is rather unusual as it's made from brown sandstone, which is not native to northern New England. It is believed that the stone was made in Connecticut and shipped to York by boat. The carving of the somber-faced angel ascending through the arches of heaven is quite striking. There is also a variety of early eighteenth-century gravestones with winged skulls and some with skulls and crossbones. Those grim images were to serve as a reminder of death. When standing in front of a winged soul (sometimes known as a soul effigy or death's head), one was to ponder one's own existence on earth and the notion of knowing that death could happen at any time.

The cemetery also has a host of unique sassafras trees that are numbered with metal tags and are on a special Maine tree registry. The trees are not native to New England and generally prefer warmer climates; however, these are some of the tallest sassafras trees on record. Perhaps the decay and decomposition of the remains in the cemetery are providing just the right amount of fertilizer to keep the trees healthy. The leaves of the trees could be mashed up to make healing balms or ointments, and once dried, the leaves were used to make sassafras tea.

There have been legends of shadow people in the cemetery who appear after dark, and there was the notion that they would only appear on the night before a death in town was to take place. Many visitors to the burial ground have told stories of hearing footsteps behind them as they walk the grounds unaccompanied. Inquisitive people seeking ghosts often take pictures of the burial ground hoping to catch a glimpse of a wandering spirit. Well-defined orbs (believed to be spiritual energy), as well as streaks of mysterious light, have been captured by some.

At the back of the cemetery is the Emerson Wilcox House, which is surrounded by a few ancient maple trees that have stood witness to the countless burials that have taken place over the years. One tree in particular continues to grow right over and around one very thick gravestone. The stone may no longer be visible after the next one hundred years. There are a handful of noticeable fieldstone markers in the burial ground; some have the scratching of crude attempts at inscriptions.

Reverend Samuel Moody and his son, Joseph (who was immortalized in Nathaniel Hawthorne's story "The Black Veil"), often attended to people on their deathbeds, giving the families comfort during difficult times. Reverend Moody had a particular phrase he used when someone died. He would say that "they were taken by death." Maybe the spirits of some of those people in York's history who were "taken by death" continue to live on and can be found in the Old York Burial Ground.

MYSTERIES AND LEGENDS

Obe's Ghost Lights

York

Standing on Dover Bluffs in Cape Neddick, one has a sweeping panoramic view of Long Sands Beach. The bluffs are quite steep, reaching sixty feet at their height, and are composed of wave-swept rocks. The name Dover Bluffs comes from the row of summer cottages on the cliffs that were once owned by people from Dover, New Hampshire. The bluffs eventually lead down toward the Nubble Lighthouse.

In the mid-1800s, Dover Bluffs was owned by a man named Obediah Stover, and the area was known as Obe's Bank, or Stover's Bank. During those years and for a time afterward, there were tales of strange lights wandering up and down the bank and through the adjacent farm fields. The lights were known as Obe's lights, and many locals were quite fascinated by them. The origins of the lights are attached to a local legend. It was said that a peddler stayed overnight at a nearby home and was never seen again. Some people believed he wandered into an abandoned cellar hole that was eventually filled in. The peddler's ghost was said to wander with a candle, looking for his missing body.

While the beautiful Nubble Lighthouse has been standing on Cape Neddick since 1879, there was a time when the locals came out to see Obe's ghost lights just down the bottom of the hill.

Those who were more skeptical at the time believed that there was a logical explanation for the ghostly lights. The gases released from decaying fish in the nearby swamp were cited as a possible source of the strange illuminations. The foxes that wandered the shore searching for food would carry the glowing fish back to their dens. It was believed that a phosphorescent glow, also known as will-o'-the-wisp, could be seen at the water's edge. Yet despite all of these explanations, there was no one to investigate the truth of the matter.

A local practical joker named Oliver Bowden had a lot of fun with the legend. He strung a long fishing line and a pulley between two trees in a nearby field. He rigged up a lantern and ran it from one tree to the other, creating the illusion of a floating "ghost light." He was able to keep this secret for many years, and during that time, there were many who were certain that they were seeing Obe's lights. Some people were so frightened that they didn't investigate further for fear of being taken away by a gruesome specter.

Oliver has since passed on, and there are now hundreds of houses throughout Cape Neddick. All the farm fields are gone. Perhaps the ghost has found what he was looking for because there haven't been any more sightings of Obe's lights by the current generation of residents.

Keeping the Peace

Wells

The beautiful Webhannet River in Wells, Maine, invites canoeists and kayakers to explore the surrounding tidal marshes. Bird and wildlife viewing is also a major attraction to visitors and day-trippers. However, back in the mid-seventeenth century, people would assemble along the scenic river to view something a bit more unusual. Constructed next to the river was a large ducking stool used to keep the peace between many residents in town. The ducking stool was essentially an instrument of social humiliation. The device was similar to a teeter-totter with a bucket seat on one end over the water. The offender would be tied to the chair and would be plunged into the icy cold river—usually several times.

The ducking stool was used most often for wives who proved to be a bother to their husbands by nagging them or not living up to what were believed to be their wifely duties. Village gossips who spent too much time involved in other people's business were also subjected to the same punishment. The ducking stool proved most effective during the cold weather months. Many residents of the village came out to watch the spectacle, and the ducking stool was believed to have kept domestic matters calm without the use of the court system.

People used to gather along the Webhannet River in Wells to watch local troublemakers being dunked into the water on the ducking stool.

The Haunting of Bryant's Hollow

Shapleigh

It was 1801. Thomas Jefferson was president of the United States, and Shapleigh, Maine, was a quiet pioneer town. Many of the settlers of the day were woodsmen, and they worked hard to clear the land and build their homes in the shadows of the wilderness and wild animals. People didn't leave the town or travel for basic needs as they grew much of what they needed right on their farms.

Mysteries and Legends

Reverend Bryant was a traveling Baptist preacher who lived in a small settlement on the Ossipee River thirty miles north of the Shapleigh Plains. He traveled by horseback, preaching the Word of God to the people. Reverend Bryant was also a peddler and carried a variety of hard-to-find supplies, such as medicine, needles and kitchenware. The roads into Shapleigh weren't much more than well-trod cow paths. The trees in places were quite thick and the roads nearly impassable due to the surrounding overgrowth. Despite the challenges Reverend Bryant often experienced in his travels, he had a dedication to his position that could not be deterred.

It was said that there was something else at work that helped ease Reverend Bryant's travels. He had a penchant for deeply sampling the rum bottle. Some men in the communities he visited secretly disliked him because when they would come home from working, their rum jugs were empty. Many hospitable womenfolk would make sure that the reverend was well stocked with rum for his travels, and sometimes that meant emptying out their husbands' stores.

On a chilly autumn day, Reverend Bryant arrived in the Shapleigh settlement at the head of the Mousam River. Both horse and rider had grown weary of their long journey, and they were ready to rest for the night. The reverend decided to spend the night at the inn, which was owned by Mr. and Mrs. Joseph Hasty. In the morning when he awoke, anxious to get an early start, Mr. Hasty advised him that the roads had changed a bit since his last visit. Reverend Bryant was told that the winding road through the plains might cause some confusion and could cause him to get lost. Mr. Hasty offered to accompany the reverend and went off to saddle both of their horses. They rode off toward the plains with a cascade of golden leaves falling around them.

Many days later, Mr. Day and Deacon Hill assembled a group of pioneers to hear the preaching of Reverend Bryant. The group became impatient after waiting for hours, but the reverend failed to appear. Many of those in attendance had brought families and food for the day. No one liked the idea of traveling home long distances in the dark as the shadows of the evening appeared. But by day's end, the only person to arrive was a messenger sent by Reverend Bryant's family. The reverend's mother and sisters had become distraught and worried about his safety since they had not seen him for days.

Although the messenger continued his search for the missing preacher, years passed, and there was neither word nor evidence to lead to his whereabouts. Those who knew the reverend held out hope, and he wasn't forgotten. Then one day, a riderless horse showed up in Shapliegh, raising concerns because it looked just like the reverend's horse. It wasn't long before the neighbors of Mr. Hasty became suspicious of him. Mrs. Hasty had inadvertently mentioned that she found a hat and a bundle that looked like the preacher's. It was rather strange because she said she found them weeks after the reverend's stay, and she knew he had had them in his possession when he bid her goodbye. All of a sudden, she stopped talking about the incident, and many believed that her husband had something to do with her silence.

Frightening tales were soon spreading throughout Shapleigh village. An unusual occurrence happened around dusk; travelers were being thrown off of their horses in an area of the plains that is now known as Bryant's Hollow. A man named Joe was visiting the village, and before he knew it, the moon was rising against the twilight sky. His ride home seemed uneventful; that is, until he reached the haunted road into the hollow. All of a sudden, Joe's horse reared back, almost throwing him into the brush. Joe steadied himself on the horse and urged it onward, but the horse would not take one step further. Spooked, the horse acted nervous. Joe dismounted and calmed the trembling horse. As he looked deeper into the hollow, he saw a figure emerge from the shadows. A man dressed in a gray coat and no hat approached him.

An ice-cold breeze seemed to cut right through Joe, and he started to speak to the figure before him. With a shaking voice, he demanded to know why this man in gray was blocking the road and wouldn't let him continue. The man in gray spoke in reassuring tones and told Joe that he didn't mean him any harm, but he did have a message to relay. Meanwhile, Joe's horse seemed to quiet down and began to munch on the grass at the edge of the road. The man told Joe that he was the first person who had been unafraid to speak to him; most people ran away. He wanted to explain why he had troubled so many travelers along the road.

It was revealed that in life he was known as Clergyman Bryant and had preached the gospel throughout the area. He relayed the story that he had last traveled the road with Joseph Hasty, with whom he had spent the previous night. As they rose through the hollow, a man named Warren emerged from the woods. The reverend explained that Warren was a man who wasn't interested in listening to the teachings of the Bible. Warren took Hasty aside, and in their whisperings, the reverend overheard them plotting against him. The men believed that the reverend was carrying money. The preacher insisted that he only carried the word of the Bible.

Just then, the voice of the reverend rose in great distress, and the specter pointed to one of the large roadside trees. The letter *B* had been carved near the bottom. Oddly, no one who had passed by the tree had cared to notice. The voice continued on, claiming that he was murdered beneath that tree. Joe looked at the tree, horrified.

The apparition asked Joe to follow him so that he could show him where his body was buried. Joe followed after the spirit through the thick oak trees and the dried leaves underfoot—the only footsteps he heard were his own. They walked several rods from the road. The reverend pointed to the ground and told Joe that this was the lonely spot where his body was buried. He suggested that Joe break off some tree branches so that he could find the spot again, and he also advised him to read the sixty-ninth Psalm to know what was going through his mind while at the hands of his attackers. The spirit told Joe that he would be able to rest now that he had told his story. When Joe was done breaking off a handful of branches, he turned to look for the apparition, but it was completely gone. Joe's fright came back as he looked around, and he noticed that it had gotten quite dark. The shadows seemed so close. He quickly scrambled out of the trees and back to the road as he tried to escape the feelings of dread.

Joe's horse moved at a quickened pace as he raced home that night, and upon arrival, he asked his mother to read him the sixty-ninth Psalm. His mother was amazed for Joe had never spent much time reading the Bible, but something about him seemed different that night. After reading the Psalm, Joe seemed to calm down a bit, and he relayed the story of his encounter with the apparition of the reverend earlier that night. His mother became excited by the story he told, and she went into detail about what she knew of the reverend's story. She also described the strange way that Mr. Hasty had acted after the disappearance. The man seemed frightened of everything; he wouldn't even milk his cows alone after dark. Those who attended his death said that he was shockingly afraid right up until the second he died.

Joe was curious if his mother knew anything of Mr. Hasty's accomplice, Warren. She had heard the gossip that linked him to the disappearance, although no one could prove anything. Coincidentally, during Warren's last days on earth, he was also overtaken by a terrifying fear, and just three days before he died he called for the local minister. It was believed that just before he died he made a confession under the promise of secrecy, and this seemed to ease his soul.

The tale of Joe's spectral encounter spread quickly through the village, but it was some time before he ventured back to the hollow. By the time he did, the area was so trampled over that he couldn't find any of the branches he had broken on that fateful night. Most people agreed that it was best not to disturb the grave of the reverend and that he should be left at peace. From that day forward, the stories of unusual encounters in the hollow came to and end.

The story doesn't end there, however. Reverend Bryant's sister had grown old, but she was constantly plagued by strange dreams. In each dream, she was urged to take a journey in which she would be able to find the man who could tell her about the death of her brother. When his sister finally heard of Joe's encounter with the spirit in the hollow, she knew she would have to find him. The reverend's mother, who was quite old but still alive, told her daughter to have faith in her dreams. She urged her to put her trust in God to protect her on the dangerous journey to search for the man who had seen her brother.

Courageously, the reverend's sister took the journey on horseback to Shapleigh to the home of Joe and his mother. When she arrived, she asked Joe to tell her the story of his encounter with her dear brother. Once she heard the story, she said that she was at peace and that their mother could be free of her worry over her missing son. She thanked Joe and set off home with the story.

Mysteries and Legends

Much of the Shapleigh plains are still wild and wooded today, and many people believe that one day, when a cellar hole or well is dug, the bones of the reverend will be found. When that gruesome reminder is found, the story of the murdered ghost from long ago will once again echo through the village.

Fort McClary

Kittery

Located just north of the New Hampshire border, Kittery has the distinction of being the oldest town in Maine, having been incorporated in 1647. The Piscataqua River, which leads to both the Portsmouth and Kittery ports, runs right past the fort. One of Kittery's most prominent

The ghosts at historic Fort McClary in Kittery often make themselves known at sunset.

citizens, William Pepperrell, acquired a tract of land known as Battery Pasture in 1689, and a defensive position was established. The land was on a prominent high point and offered a commanding view of the harbor. It is believed that there were early structures built on the site, called Fort Pepperrell. In 1715, the Province of Massachusetts Bay voted to erect a breastwork of six guns for defense of the river. A permanent naval officer was also appointed at the fort; it was his job to collect money from all ships and vessels entering the harbor. The monies that were collected were used to purchase powder and shot for the fort.

It was believed that a new fortification was built around 1720, called Fort William in honor of its founder. During the Revolution, the Pepperrell family remained loyal to the king, and the property was confiscated. The fort was soon renamed Fort McClary, taking it's name from Andrew McClary, a New Hampshire native who was killed at the Battle of Bunker Hill. The New Hampshire Militia manned the fort until 1779, and then it was abandoned. The fort was garrisoned and rebuilt during the Civil War.

The blockhouse that currently stands in the fort was built in 1844. Vice President Hannibal Hamlin served briefly at the fort. There were a number of structures that existed during the nineteenth century, including barracks, officers' quarters, a powder magazine and two riflemen's houses. There was also a guard shack and hospital. When the war ended, the fort fell into severe disrepair. The property was purchased from Massachusetts in 1924. During World War I and World War II, the site was used as a lookout, but by that time it had been replaced by Fort Foster out on Kittery Point. In addition to the hexagonal blockhouse, there is a brick powder magazine structure that dates to 1808. There is also an immense, unfinished granite wall that dates back to the nineteenth century. Foundations of buildings and underground tunnels can also be found on the property.

Many visitors enjoy bringing picnics and catching an occasional sea breeze. Ghostly encounters at the fort typically happen at sunset, just before the park closes. One story concerns a woman who visited the fort to take pictures of Portsmouth Harbor Lighthouse just across the water in New Castle, New Hampshire. After the sun went down, the park became dark very quickly as she was making her way back to the parking lot. When she stepped off the path back onto the gravel lot, she realized that she was the last one to leave. Quickening her pace toward her car, she was stopped in her tracks by something that looked like car headlights coming through the trees to her right. It seemed quite strange, as there was no road or houses in that direction. Frozen with shock, she stood still until she could see a silhouette in the light—it was the shape of a woman. The figure almost appeared to be coming right out of the trees. The woman said that she didn't feel afraid but felt that there was an almost angelic essence to the spirit in front of her.

What seemed like an eternity was most likely just a few minutes as, speechless, the woman stared at the figure in the trees, wondering what was going to happen next. All of a sudden, the light began to dim, and the silhouette started to disappear. The woman looked around the parking lot to see if there was anyone else around, but there was still no one. Within moments, the light was gone. The woman found herself standing in the dark shadow of the trees as stars started to peek out of the indigo sky above. Back in her car, the woman sat for a moment running the encounter through her mind, trying to make sense of it. But she couldn't. She drove home believing that what she saw was most definitely a ghost.

A man visiting the fort also told stories of seeing ghostly entities just after the sun went down. He was down along the stone wall by the water when he looked back up and saw shadowy figures in what appeared to be military uniforms walking between the remaining structures. He ran toward the hill, hoping to get a closer look, and as he ascended the stairs next to the blockhouse, he saw the uniformed figure disappear near the powder house. He then looked toward the foundation of one of the barracks buildings and caught a quick flash of the building still standing there, complete and intact. There was another figure in a military uniform that disappeared into the building and vanished, and once again there was nothing but the usual foundation in this spot.

Fort McClary is almost as old as the town of Kittery itself. It is a great place to visit for those who want to learn of the local history. If you dare to stay at the fort until sunset, you may be greeted by some of the spirits who wait until the twilight hours to make their appearance to visitors.

Old Gaol/King's Prison

York

Looming rather large and imposing on a stone hill is the Old Gaol, also known as the King's Prison. The original gaol was built along Meetinghouse Creek in 1656, just three years after it was agreed that a royal prison was required for the Province of Maine. It was later decided to move the structure to its current location. Timbers from the original structure were used in the construction, and the building was ready to accept prisoners in 1719.

Stepping over the threshold is like stepping back two hundred years, and the modern world outside seems to disappear. The kitchen of the gaoler's quarters warrants much interest, as it looks much like it did in the eighteenth century: simple and somewhat primitive. The old wooden ceiling beams above seem dark and weathered, having absorbed the scent of many meals prepared in the room over the years. A massive oak door about eighteen inches thick can be found at one end of the room, and it opens to the entrance to the old dungeon. A noticeable chill can be felt crossing into this ominous room, and one can't help but

Once known as the King's Prison, the Old Gaol is one of the oldest surviving British public buildings in the United States.

wonder how the dungeon stayed warm on the coldest of winter days. The walls feel close, and the sense of light and freedom seem far away after just a few minutes of standing in the room. The stone floor radiates the temperature of the earth beneath. Many prisoners must have sat and looked at this very floor for days, weeks or longer.

The second floor of the gaol seems a little brighter, although there is a large iron ring set in the center of the floor where prisoners were chained.

In June 1790, eight prisoners, believed to have had outside assistance, escaped. Later that year, on the night of September 3, 1790, five prisoners escaped from the gaol by cutting off one of the grates in one of the dungeon rooms. In March 1819, another daring but bloody escape took place. There was a grate through which food would be placed; the edges were surrounded by sharp saw blades as a deterrent to escape. Witnesses of the scene couldn't comprehend how the prisoner could have escaped without fatally injuring himself. Shortly after the prisoner's daring escape, he was recaptured and questioned about how he did it. He said that he had greased himself up and slipped through to the next cell, which was unoccupied and whose door was open. While the man had several cuts from passing between the saw blades, none of his injuries proved life threatening. Surprisingly, upon closer look, the man seemed to have an odd-shaped flat head, along with a very slim build, characteristics that helped him escape.

Some of the more dangerous inmates, hardened criminals and some murderers, were shipped off to prisons in Massachusetts or sent to the newly established state prison in Thomaston after 1824. Nearly half of those incarcerated in the early nineteenth century were debtors. They could be imprisoned by their creditors almost indefinitely while their debts were outstanding. If the creditor could not prove that the debtor was capable of paying his debt, the debtor would only spend thirty days in jail. Debtors often had to wait for the creditors to grow tired of paying for their incarceration in order to be released.

Some of the other offenses committed by the prisoners at the gaol included gossip, counterfeiting, failure to keep the Sabbath, abuse, adultery, profanity and assault. A law in 1820 against gross lewdness encompassed everything from adultery to prostitution, and the sentence was outlined that the violator would be punished by solitary imprisonment for a term not exceeding three months and hard labor not exceeding five years. It was also noted that between 1801 and 1830, eleven men were identified as "deranged" or "mad," and they were also imprisoned at the gaol.

One of the most famous prisoners at the gaol was Patience Boston, an Indian servant from Nauset, Cape Cod, Massachusetts. She was a Christian convert who once attended church in her hometown regularly. She was imprisoned in the winter of 1734 for the murder of Benjamin Trot of Falmouth in Casco Bay, a child of about eight years of age whom she drowned in a well on July 9, 1734. When she was jailed, she was pregnant, a condition that lengthened her stay until she gave birth to her child. She had been accused of abusing her husband, drunkenness and arson. Reverend Samuel Moody took credit for Patience accepting her sins after he spent extensive time with her in prison. She was hanged on July 31, 1735, on the gallows were where the Stage Neck Inn now stands. Her child was adopted by local residents.

Gallows Point was described as a place where hundreds of people would come out to see the prisoners "kick the beam." The structure consisted of an upright beam with another beam extending from it. A narrow platform stood six or seven feet below the beam and could be reached by climbing a ladder. The rope suspended from the beam was adjusted, and the victim was pushed or kicked off the platform. Sometimes the body would swing back, and the legs would "kick the beam," much to the delight of the crowd.

The gaol eventually became the county jail and then served as a school and boardinghouse until it was abandoned in the 1890s. A movement to save the historic structure was begun, and with the assistance of the recently formed Old York Historical and Improvement Society, the building was restored and opened as a museum in 1900. Many luminary citizens of the day attended the July 1 dedication, including noted author Mark Twain.

There are a few stories that the building can be a creepy place to be a tour guide or interpreter, as some folks believe that the building is haunted by the spirit of Patience Boston. A handful of people have commented on sensing another presence in the gaol. One of the windows to the jail is often found mysteriously open in the middle of the night, when no one is around. Visitors to the Old Gaol can't resist climbing in the replica stocks out in front for pictures. Those visitors might want to take a look over their shoulders just to make sure there isn't a ghostly visitor from the past peering out of an open window of the oldest jail in the country, watching them.

SACO RIVER CURSE

Saco

The legend of an old Indian curse still lingers throughout the community of Saco today. Many people believe that the curse has continued to come to pass over hundreds of years, while others believe that it is just a tale of warning. In 1675, there was a tragic encounter between English sailors and a Sokoki Indian squaw and child. The location of the incident was on Factory Island, once known as Indian Island, along the Saco River.

An Indian woman with a baby was crossing the river in a canoe when she was spotted by the sailors. The men were believed to have indulged in a large share of rum that night, and they felt that they had something to prove. They wanted to test the theory that was commonly believed by white men: Indian children were said to be able to swim instinctively from birth, like wild animals. They upset the canoe, much to the horror of the Indian woman. The baby sank to the bottom of the river quickly, and although its mother kept diving to save the child, it was too late. She finally recovered the baby's body and brought it to shore. It was reported that the child died as a result of his submersion in the ice-cold water.

The Indian squaw wasn't just anyone; she was Nibena, wife of Squando, chief and high priest of the Sokoki tribe. He took the attack on his child with great pain, and the harmony amongst the white settlers along the river was threatened. On September 18, 1675, Squando launched an all-out attack on the settlers in Saco. The settlers heard from an Indian informant of the impending attack, and that gave them time to retreat to the garrison house of Major William Philips. While the attack by Squando was swift, it wasn't successful. Over the next seventy-five years, the settlers and Indians suffered great adversity. Peace treaties were signed, but in the end the Sokokis moved away from the Saco River.

It was said that Squando cursed the river to claim the lives of three white men every year until all the white men had fled the river's banks. The river originates deep in the White Mountains of New Hampshire and spans three Maine counties. Measuring 140 miles, the strong currents of the Saco River have claimed hundreds of lives over the years. In 1978, Maine's Warden Service confirmed getting at least three or four drowning incidents per year. When the first drowning of the year happened, people knew that it would be the first of many.

Some people believe that the curse was a made-up addition to the original story that happened in 1675; however, the accidents on the river seem to be consistent with the curse. Many generations of parents have told their children of the Saco River curse in order to keep their children away from the rushing waters. While the Sokoki tribe may be no more, many believe that the legendary curse will remain as long as the waters of the river continue to flow.

The Ghostly Child of Zion's Hill

Kennebunk

Scenic Summer Street is filled with a wonderful collection of antique ships' captain's homes, and each house has a wonderful story to tell. In the late 1800s, there was a tragic day on the hill that has now turned into local legend. A young boy was playing with a ball, unaware that a team of horses pulling a wagon was heading up the hill. The ball rolled into the street as the boy chased after it, and there was no time for the horses to stop. The ball rolled down the hill and came to rest on the doorstep of one of the old homes. The young boy had been killed instantly.

Many years after the tragic event, local residents claimed to have heard the sound of horses' hooves coming up the hill, but there were no horses.

Some people also spoke of seeing a ghostly ball rolling across the street, down the hill and disappearing after it came to rest on a doorstep. The story is thought to replay itself over, like a psychic impression caught in a continuous loop.

The Devil's Invention

York

In July of 1679, James Adams of York had several disagreements and arguments with his neighbor, Henry Simpson. One day, James had had enough of dealing with his neighbor, so he thought up some sort of revenge to put their issues to an end. According to reports, his plans were not only deliberate but also considered "satanical." In an isolated area about four or five miles away from the village, James built a holding pen out of rocks and logs. It was several feet in height, and the walls were on an incline inward from bottom to top.

James decided to use Henry Simpson's two children, ages six and nine, as decoys. He lured them into the woods toward the holding pen under the pretense of looking for birds' nests. He tricked them into going into the pen, where he confined them in hopes that they would perish from famine. It wasn't long before the children were reported missing, and a forty-eight-hour search ensued. The two children became frightened as time passed, and they realized that they needed to find a way out of the trap they were in. The children clawed and dug at the earth around the logs at the base of the pen and eventually escaped.

The boys wandered through the woods for the next three days, following the noise of the seashore, where they were eventually found. The locals named the location where the boys were kept prisoner the Devil's Invention. James was detained, and his punishment was thirty deep lashes with a whip, along with paying the father of the children five pounds and the treasurer ten pounds and jail fees. Eventually, James was taken twenty-one days' distance out of York and never returned.

Hackmatack Playhouse

Berwick

A weatherworn red barn in Berwick, Maine, at the edge of a spacious farm field is often busy with activity. Lights go out, figures step out of the darkness and people come from all around to see what's going to happen next. The music starts to play, and from the shadows costumed actors emerge. Are these ghosts from the past? Actually, they are performers getting ready to bring a little bit of Broadway to one of New England's most unique theaters, the Hackmatack Playhouse.

The wonderful venue, which offers performances by both local and New York actors, is one of the best reasons to visit this old seventeenth-century farm turned summer theater; to learn the history and sneak a peek at the ghostly legends are other reasons. The interior of the antique

Are ghostly actors and actresses still attracted to the stage of the Hackmatack Playhouse in North Berwick, Maine?

Mysteries and Legends

Ghostly specters have been seen in the old barn that houses the playhouse's vast collection of costumes.

dairy barn offers a stage, rows of seating and overhead stage lights. Along the wooden walls are hand-painted planks with the names of the former residents of the barn: the cows (Dottie, Ethel and Lil). The building is comfortably equipped with 218 seats salvaged from a Durham, New Hampshire movie theater. The playhouse has its own special mystique, and it's easy to let the imagination wander throughout every nook and cranny of the old building.

The stories of ghosts are most likely linked to the first settlement of the farm and the generations of descendants who have maintained it over the last three hundred years. Michael Guptill is proud of his family's heritage, and he is eager to offer details on the history of the two-hundred-acre farm. In the mid-1600s, the original "Gubtails" moved from the British Isles to settle in the area. The first house that was built was described as a log home, originally set on the far left back of the property. Indian raids were fairly frequent throughout much of the late seventeenth and eighteenth centuries in the area, which was known as the Salmon Falls region. Sadly, it was during one of these attacks, according to family history, that their ancestors were killed and the first house was burned to the ground.

A new Cape-style farmhouse was built in 1716. At one time, the house was occupied by two Guptill brothers, and an interesting conversation came up one day between them. One brother wanted a more modern, two-story Cape, while the other thought the house was plenty good enough the way it was. However, the younger brother declared, "My half is coming off"—and he proceeded to saw his half of the house off and tear it down. He then built on to the end of the original house a two-story Cape, parallel to the road. Although additions to the house have been made as recently as 2005, it still retains all of the charm of a quaint old New England farmhouse.

The barn has its own interesting history. The original barn was struck by lightning and burned down in 1934. It was thought that the heat from the newly harvested hay might have attracted the lightning. A new barn was located to serve as the replacement; however, moving it to its current location proved to be a bit challenging. The barn was across the street from the Guptill Farm. It measured fifty-four feet long and forty-two feet wide and had pegged timbers. Instead of disassembling the barn and reconstructing it, the decision was made to jack the barn up on rollers and attach cables to it. A cable ran through a turnstile, and an old white horse was hitched up to turn it. With each step of the horse, the turnstile would move the barn. It was quite a slow process, and when the horse completed the circle, the barn would move only a half inch. In the end, it took three days and the crossing of a major road before it reached its destination.

Generations of entertainers were in the Guptill family, including Michael's grandfather, Lewis Guptill, the state's grange master, who played six instruments. Michael's father, Carleton, was interested in theater, and he took some courses while attending agricultural school at the University of Maine in the early 1950s. Michael has a wonderful collection of photos reflecting his family's involvement in these pursuits.

However, as the 1950s wore on, being a dairy farmer became quite a challenge. The needs and expenses of the farm made it extremely difficult to make money. Carleton decided that he would become a teacher, and he ended up selling the last of his cows about the same time he became director of the drama department at the Oyster River High School. With a revitalized role in theater, he decided to convert the barn into the Hackmatack Playhouse in 1972. A handful of updates to the barn were needed, such as reinforcing the roof, a concrete floor and the installation of rows of seats. However, the theater still very much resembles an old dairy barn; that is, until the actors take the stage.

There are several other buildings on the property, including an old carriage house and an old mill building that was once used as a sawmill. This fascinating structure still has the antique metal pulleys overhead that were used to drive the saws. Underfoot are worn, wooden floorboards that flex and bend just slightly when trod upon. Signs for past theater performances surround workbenches, tools and buckets of paint. There have been stories from those who pass through the building of hearing the mill equipment running at full speed, although much of the equipment hasn't been used for years and is covered by a thick layer of dust. After climbing the old wooden staircase in the back of the building, a step into the attic brings visitors into another world.

Up here, there are endless racks of costumes and clothing that extend the entire length of the building. Shelves surround the room, with piles of blue jeans and dress pants from every era and in every size. From wedding gowns to flapper dresses and military uniforms, the variety of costumes is quite extensive. Lining the base of the aisles are curious, large trunks, some with words and stickers from their various travels. Each trunk is filled with everything from hats to gloves. Everything is well organized, and there is actually a map of the attic detailing where various items are for easy reference. Windows at either end of the attic let in the natural light during the day, but one can only imagine what happens after the sun has gone down and the costumes take on their own eerie qualities under the fluorescent light. Some who have visited the attic have described feeling another presence in the room and sometimes seeing someone dart between the aisles from the corners of their eyes. Are they ghostly spirits of actors past, still looking for their costumes as they prepare for another performance? Perhaps.

The woodshed, which was once the slaughterhouse, is one of the oldest buildings on the property and is used by the actors to rehearse and develop their characters. A variety of props are stored there as well. Unseen voices calling out visitors' names have been heard when the building is completely empty. Even sounds from the occasional farm animal have been heard from time to time, yet there are none present.

The theater, of course, is said to have its own share of activity. Visitors, and even some members of the production crew, have felt that they were not alone. The coveted seats closest to the stage seem to have the most noticeable areas of energy. A couple of stories tell of full-bodied apparitions that seem to disappear right before one's eyes in the theater. One of the ghosts is believed to be a Native American spirit that dates back to the 1600s, during the time of the Indian disputes.

Even the old eighteenth-century farmhouse is believed to have its own spirited activity. Michael Guptill is open minded about the ghostly activity as he continues the rich tradition of maintaining the family farm. If you decide to visit the Hackmatack Playhouse, be sure to try one of the delicious homemade fresh fruit desserts (before they are sold out). Also, make certain that you leave an extra seat beside you in the theater for one of its many spirited inhabitants.

The Hurd Manor/Angel of the Berwicks

North Berwick

The director of the Maine Historic Preservation Commission called Hurd Manor "the most outstanding example of its style in southern Maine and nowhere in the state does a more impressive Queen Anne–Eastlake residence exist." Not only is the house impressive, but also the story of the tenacious and accomplished woman who built it is equally fascinating. Mary Hurd was born into a Quaker family on March 27, 1839, in North Berwick. Mary's father, William "Friend" Hill, was a leader of the Quaker Church and a leading citizen and businessman. Mary was one of twelve

The stunning architecture and history of the Hurd Manor in North Berwick, Maine, has earned the house the distinction of being called the finest Queen Anne–style Victorian house in the state.

children. Sadly, eight of them died early in their youths. It was thought that some of the children may have died from lead poisoning. Lead paint was used by wealthier families (the poor used lead-free whitewash). Even as a young woman, Mary renounced the Quaker style of dress for fashions more of the nineteenth century. She even joined the Free Will Baptist Church only a short distance from where she was born.

Mary's mother, Elizabeth Buffum Hill, died in 1859, when Mary was just twenty years old. Daniel Hurd, a local man, became Mary's love interest, and she went to her father to tell him of her intentions. Mary's father felt that Daniel was a drunkard, a gambler and a carouser and that he would not be a suitable husband for her. In fact, her father is reported to have said, "If thee wants a husband I shall get thee one." Mary's father had worked his way up the ranks, eventually gaining ownership at the local woolen mill, and he thought one of the men there would be perfect for Mary. William Hobbs was treasurer and agent of the mill, and he was also a widower with two young daughters. Mary put aside her love for Daniel and agreed to marry William as her father wished.

A simple house was built next to her father's home, and it was presented to Mary and William as a wedding gift. Mary raised both of the young girls and was a good wife to William. In 1881, Mary's father died, and he left her control of the North Berwick Mill Company. Mary's husband died the following year after a long debilitating illness. Mary's life changed after the deaths of the two important men in her life. She hired architects to move the house her father gave her and build a new house attached to the front of it. This new house boasted six thousand square feet and was everything a Quaker-style house was not. The house had hand-carved oak doors, a black walnut staircase and banister, hand-painted friezes, a granite foundation and soaring brick chimneys. Some of the details of the house are extremely unique, including a gray marble fireplace with thousands of ancient fossils, from trilobites to worms, embedded in it. There are faces in the façade of the house that include Boreas, the Greek god of the north wind, and Baccus the Greek god of wine and fertility.

Mary's first love, Daniel Hurd, bided his time during the years of her marriage, and he was still available after the death of her husband and father. Daniel was fifty-three and Mary was fifty-four when they were finally married in 1893—a dream come true for the both of them. He moved into the beautiful Queen Anne Victorian, which became known as Hurd Manor. A respected businessman, Hurd became a state senator, although he still loved farming. When his term in office ended, he became president of the North Berwick Bank (which he and Mary built and founded) in 1923. Mary ran the mill to the highest of standards, with very few accidents and without the use of child labor, which was common at the time. The Hurds also owned two large, black, twelve-cylinder Packards, in which they were often chauffeured throughout town. The couple had also become civic leaders in their community, and they were involved in many charitable causes. The Daniel Hurd Library in town was built with funds from the Hurd family, and there is a large portrait of Daniel in the front of the building. Mary built a fire station and purchased a fire truck for the town.

In August 1931, during the centennial celebration in town, the Hurds were heralded by Governor William Gardiner for all their accomplishments. It was just a few months later, in December 1931, that Daniel Hurd died rather suddenly. He was followed by Mary less than two years later. The pallbearers at her funeral represented her life: two men from her household, two men from the mill and two firemen. Mary and Daniel were laid to rest at the Mount Pleasant Cemetery, in the family burial plot of her first husband.

The house was empty and abandoned for about ten years after the deaths of the Hurds. Eventually, it was sold off for a number of different business ventures. Over the years, the twenty-five-room house has been everything from a boardinghouse and apartment building to a restaurant, tavern, real estate office and law practice. There were whispers in town that the house was cursed and that no business would be successful there. For a time, the house was quite shabby and rough looking. It was written about the house that "it needed to be loved to respond in kind." Many residents had hoped that a business would outlast the curse, and just as it seemed that the latest owners would stay and maintain the house, they moved on. The incredible house required a varying amount of repairs over the years. Broken windows would have to be sent to West Virginia to be repaired due to their thickness and handmade nature. One of the owners of the property was interviewed by a newspaper reporter after purchasing the house, and he was quoted in saying that he had hoped the house was haunted by ghosts.

In 2005, the house was purchased by Sally McLaren and Ben Gumm, a couple that had extensive experience owning and operating a bed-and-breakfast. They had a vision for the property to bring back the elegance of the Victorian house, and they renamed the property Angel of the Berwicks. A four-year renovation and restoration was undertaken to update the building and to showcase some of the grandeur of the mansion. The building went from yellow to mulberry with plum trim. During the renovations, a stairway to nowhere was discovered behind a door that was an abandoned design for a back hall staircase concealed in a closet. A large nineteenth-century, custom-built safe in a wooden cabinet that looked brand new was part of the architecture of the house as well. The property was opened as an inn, and it began attracting regular guests from all over the country. The bridal suite is one of the largest rooms in the house, and from the window one can look down the hill at the old mill complex.

The details of the house are amazing, and it's almost impossible to believe that the woman who designed the house grew up with a Quaker upbringing. It seems as though the house is enjoying its recent revival—it hasn't looked better in years. Perhaps the whispered curse has finally been put to rest now that the house is given the love that it needs.

The Lost Village of Tatnic Hill

Wells

The farming village of Tatnic Hill is only a memory now, but it was once part of Wells, Maine, bordered by the eastern edge of South Berwick. The village was first occupied by homesteaders in the late 1700s. It has been called the "area of the seven wonders." There was a natural spring at a crossroads in the village and natural stone caves in the rock formations that may have once provided refuge from Indian attacks. The "Balancing Rock" was an unusual rock formation that had become quite a local curiosity. A steep waterfall named Orris Falls offered a cooling cascade of water in one area of the settlement.

There aren't many remnants of the original village that once stood in the young woods, except for cellar holes and stone walls. The location is quite isolated and has sometimes been referred to as a "backwoods" place. Without a map in hand, one could get lost pretty quickly. The sad thing about the history of the village is that the homesteaders who lived there sealed the village's fate to become abandoned. Those who settled in Tatnic were desperate for any kind of land they could obtain, and they were willing to do whatever it took to make it livable.

The land was not ideal for homesteading, and those who worked on the hill overcame a lot of odds to cut down the trees and build their homes. The soil was shallow and rocky, so trying to plant fields of crops was quite difficult. The only plants that would take root were beans and Indian corn. During the early days of the settlement, the future seemed to hold some promise, as many of the trees were felled for logging. As time went on, young trees began to take over the small farm fields. Stone walls that had been built were not sufficient for keeping livestock. In the mid-1800s, younger generations were seeking more promising opportunities outside of the village in nearby Wells. Struggling hay fields were finally abandoned, and hardwood trees grew in those spaces.

The houses that were built when the settlement began were nearing one hundred years old in the late nineteenth century, and many of them needed repair. The expenses to maintain the houses became too much for the homesteaders to bear. The winters on the hill were progressively becoming more difficult to weather. As the elders in the community began to age and pass on, the houses started to become empty, one by one left to the elements. In the late 1800s, the last family left Tatnic Hill. In the early twentieth century, few logging efforts were made on the abandoned property. During the 1920s, there was a brief effort at quarrying some of the ledge rock, but it was finished almost as soon as it began. The small amounts of rock that were being obtained didn't seem to be worth the effort to the quarrying companies.

The remains of the homes disintegrated, and pine trees grew up through chimneys and old barn walls. A moss-covered cemetery can also be found along the hill, bearing the names of the original inhabitants of Tatnic. The town of Wells gave up the village as "abandoned" and no longer maintained the narrow dirt roads that led to the hill. The location became a haven for those with off-road vehicles who rode through the village, further pushing the history and old home foundations deeper into the ground. The property is currently owned by the Great Works Land

Trust, and for those adventurous souls who are seeking the past, it's a bit of a climb through the woods to get there.

There are reminders of the village underfoot and behind bushes and trees, although they continue to disappear with every passing year. The location is said to be a bit spooky, and nighttime visitors often lose their bearings in the dark. Trees now shadow the remnants of a community of homes that was abandoned and given back to the woods and nature.

The Sawtell Murder

Lebanon

Lebanon, Maine, is a rural town founded by farmers and lumbermen. In 1870, a railroad was built through Lebanon, and it helped the town grow and prosper. However, just twenty years later, a grisly murder rocked this quiet little town, and it took a long time for the residents to recover from the shock. The story created sensational headlines in newspapers throughout New England.

Isaac and Hiram Sawtell were brothers born in Boston, Massachusetts. Hiram was a shopkeeper, and Isaac was a dentist. On June 8, 1877, Isaac was arrested for the rape of Bessie Crotty earlier that spring. He was found guilty and sentenced to fifteen years in state prison. After serving nine months, he was brought up on charges of raping another woman, Theresa Berry, also in the spring of 1877. Isaac pleaded not guilty in both cases and accused the woman of prostitution and trying to swindle him out of $500. Nevertheless, Isaac served twelve years of his thirty-year sentence. He petitioned Governor Oliver Ames of Massachusetts on March 1, 1899, for a pardon, which was granted. Isaac's mother accompanied him to the statehouse in Boston to personally thank the governor and to tell him that Isaac had been completely rehabilitated.

Isaac returned to his mother's house and persuaded her to deed all of her property to him. Hiram argued with Isaac, and he said that he would see to it that he wouldn't get another cent. Isaac responded that he didn't

Mysteries and Legends

The horrible memory of the Sawtell murder resides somewhere in the woods of Lebanon, Maine.

want to be driven to an "extreme." The wheels were in motion, and Isaac carefully plotted out a scheme to keep his brother from interfering any further.

Isaac planned to take his mother to Lowell, and Hiram's eight-year-old daughter, Marian, was going to take the trip with them. After visiting Lowell, the group ended up in Rochester, New Hampshire, where they spent the next two nights at a boardinghouse. Isaac sent a card to Hiram telling him that his daughter was very ill. Afterward, he went to a local store to purchase a shovel and pickaxe. Later that night, Isaac took his mother and his niece for a ride and insisted that Marian drink something from a cup. Isaac had mixed something in the drink that made Marian vomit. Isaac then sent another telegram to his brother that the little girl was ill, and their mother requested him to take the train at once.

When Hiram arrived, Isaac met him at the train station in Rochester with a carriage he had rented. Their greeting was said to be cordial, and they headed off along Portland Street. Isaac turned the carriage behind a barn and fired three gunshots into Hiram as he sat beside him in the buggy. The first shot went directly into Hiram's heart, and he died instantly.

Later that night, Isaac returned to the boardinghouse, and he, Marian and his mother returned to Boston. Over the next few days, Isaac's mother became concerned over the disappearance of Hiram. Isaac agreed to take the train back to Rochester to see if he could find out if Hiram had ever arrived. He returned to Boston two days later, empty-handed. His mother accused him of murdering Hiram and said that she would have him arrested within twenty-four hours. Isaac headed back to Rochester and then, later, to Portland, Maine, where he bought a ticket on a train headed west. He was apprehended just before boarding for not paying his hotel bill.

During this time, detectives were dispatched from Boston to Rochester. A hatchet was discovered in a river, and a shopkeeper remembered selling it to Isaac. Over one hundred men were assembled to try to find Hiram's body. The man from whom Isaac had rented the horse was questioned, and the detectives decided to ride the horse and see where it led. The horse followed the lonely Marsh Road, which connected Lebanon, Maine, with

Somersworth, New Hampshire. The horse eventually led them to the spot where it had been hitched to a tree. The surrounding ground was dug up, and the body was uncovered; however, the head was missing, the arms had been cut off and all of the clothing had been removed, except for the socks. All of those steps had been taken to prevent identification of the body. A gold cuff button belonging to Isaac was found in the grave, linking him to the murder.

The body was removed, and an inquest was scheduled in East Lebanon. The body was taken to the schoolhouse in South Lebanon. Crowds had assembled at the schoolhouse. The remains were placed on two boards, and the curious could walk around the corpse and view both sides. The undertaker eventually arrived and took the body away on a carriage driven by two black horses.

An exhausting search was undertaken to find Hiram's head, but winter was bearing down, and despite well-organized efforts, there was no luck. Isaac's trial was in Dover, New Hampshire, and he was found guilty of committing the murder. He was sentenced to one year in the state prison in Concord, and on the first Tuesday in 1892, he was to be hanged by the neck until dead.

In December 1891, Isaac felt the impending doom of his sentence, and he couldn't rest. In his guilt, he confessed to further details of the murder. He drew a map of where he had buried the head in the woods in East Lebanon. Searchers found Hiram's head underneath a pile of brush and dirt. Isaac was visited by his elderly mother, and she didn't seem to fully know what was going on. On December 24, 1891, Isaac ate his lunch, but at dinner he refused to eat. Later that night, one of the prison watchmen noticed that Isaac was breathing heavily; he entered his cell and found him unconscious. The prison doctor was dispatched, and he felt that Isaac would soon be dead from apoplectic shock. The doctor tried to revive him as best he could, but he declared Isaac dead at 10:05 a.m. on December 26, 1891, just one year and one day from the date of the original conviction. Rumors circulated that perhaps Isaac's mother had slipped him some opium during her visit so that he didn't have to face the gallows. An autopsy was called for, and it was determined that a blood clot had developed in his brain, possibly brought about by anxiety.

Isaac had told his lawyer that he wanted to be buried with his brother at the Forest Hill Cemetery in Boston, but the cemetery trustees refused due to public pressure. The body was shipped from Concord via American Express to Great Falls, New Hampshire, and was put in the care of James Edgerly, the undertaker. A public uproar happened when the body was shipped to Great Falls, as no one wanted to bury the body in their public cemeteries. Days passed, and the body was guarded. One night, the body vanished. To this day, no one knows what became of it. Hiram's head was given to Isaac's lawyer to be brought to Forest Hills in Boston, but the authorities refused to have the head buried there. The whereabouts of Hiram's head today are also a mystery.

The schoolhouse in South Lebanon where Hiram's body was laid out was eventually turned into a private home. Many longtime residents in town tell stories of the house's ghostly inhabitant. Most people believe that the shadowy figure often seen in the house is the ghost of Hiram, who will never rest in peace.

Old Trickey the Sandman

York

It was the late 1600s in York, and Old Trickey was a fisherman who lived along the York River. He was described as having an irritable disposition. He often carried a Bible with him, and he was often seen talking to himself as he sat at the mouth of the York River with the book in his hand. On the rare occasion he went into town, he was always seen muttering to himself, often turning pages in the Bible as he walked.

When Trickey died, some of the locals got their hands on his Bible, and the rumor of a devil's curse was begun. It was thought that Trickey was so mean that the devil had actually cursed him with a never-ending task. The mission that Trickey had to undertake was to move sand from one side of the river to the other side, using only a singular piece of rope to complete the task. He found this to be an almost impossible

Mysteries and Legends

The John Hancock Warehouse along the York River dates from the 1740s and once belonged to the famous American Patriot. Can the voice of Old Trickey the Sandman be heard in the distance from this spot?

task, and often storms would blow around him; some thought they were summoned by the devil. Trickey would often shout, "More rope, more rope!" so that he could complete his job, although he was never supplied with any. Some mornings, the locals noticed that the sand had shifted strangely over the night, and the shifting was attributed to Old Trickey the Sandman. The legend lives on today, and many locals say that you can hear Old Trickey's voice shouting out along the York River just before a storm hits.

As for Trickey's Bible, which is now in the collection of the Old York Historical Society, some claim that it is a haunted artifact. Hundreds of years old, the book is rather dry and in rough condition, but it's said to snap shut when opened. On some occasions, it's said that the book can barely be opened. Is it Old Trickey's curse to keep people out of his belongings, or is it just a coincidence?

BIBLIOGRAPHY

Belkin, Douglas. "Local Ghostbusters Investigate the Supernatural on a Lonely, Windswept Maine Isle." *Boston Globe*, October 23, 2005.

Boston Sunday Herald. "King's Gaol at York." August 25, 1901.

Edwards, Susan C.S. "North Berwick's Architectural Grand Dame." *York County Coast Star*, February 22, 1989.

Ellis, Annie. "Ghost Hunters Descend on Wood Island: Reporter Joins Crew for Night of Ghastly Investigation." *Biddeford-Saco Courier*, October 12, 2006.

Emery, Edwin. *History of Sanford, Maine, 1661–1900*. Springvale, ME: Harland Eastman Publishers, 1987.

Emery, George Alex. *Ancient City of Gorgeana and Modern Town of York*. York, ME: York Corner Publishing, 1894.

Gilpatric, George A. *Kennebunk History*. Kennebunk, ME: Star Print Press, 1939.

Hardy, Joseph W. *Settlement and Abandonment on Tatnic Hill*. Portsmouth, NH: Back Channel Press, 2008.

Joy, Kenneth. *The Kennebunks: Out of the Past*. Freeport, ME: Bond Wheelwright Company, 1967.

Joyce, Betty. *Maine in Transition*. West Kennebunk, ME: Phoenix Publishing, 1992.

Bibliography

Kences, James E. "Overtaken by Death: Dying, Death and Burial in Early York." Occasional Paper No. 2, 1995. Old York Historical Society, York, Maine.

Kittery Bicentennial Committee. *Kittery Kaleidoscope.* Somersworth: New Hampshire Printers, 1976.

Lowe, Elwyn. *A History of Shapleigh, Maine.* Unpublished ms., 1985.

McNulty, Bryan. "Saco River Curse." *Portland Press Herald,* June 13, 1979.

Mitchell, Harry, and Edward Campbell. *The Town Register, Berwick.* Berwick, ME: H.E. Mitchell Publishing Company, 1904.

Moody, Edward C. *Handbook History of the Town of York.* Kennebec, ME: Kennebec Journal Co., 1914.

Ostrander, Kathy. *Remembering the Kennebunks.* Charleston, SC: The History Press, 2009.

Redlon, Gladys, and Leroy S. Sawtell. "Murder." Unpublished ms., 1960. Collection of the Lebanon Historical Society.

Rolde, Neil. *York Is Living History.* Brunswick, ME: Harpswell Press, 1975.

Ryan, Roberta, Mary Rogers Hurd and Doughty Falls. *History of North Berwick, Maine 1831–2006.* Portsmouth, NH: Peter Randall Publishing, 2006.

Schmidt, Henrietta. *Down to the Seas.* Kennebunk, ME: Star Press, 1977.

Shelly, Hope M., and the 350th Celebration Committee. *My Name Is Wells: I am the Town.* Penobscot, ME: Penobscot Press, 2002.

Sneddon, Rob. "Give My Regards to Berwick." *Down East Magazine* (June 2006).

Toll, Susan Leonard. "The York Gaol, 1810–1830: Deviance and Social Change." Occasional Paper No. 1, 1995. Old York Historical Society, York, Maine.

[Wells] *Weekly Sentinel.* "Hurd Manor Undergoes Renovations to Become the Angel of the Berwicks." May 5, 2006.

Winn, Ralph H. *The Maine That Was: Legends of Cape Neddick.* Freeport, ME: Bond Wheelwright Co., 1964.

York County Coast Star. "Hurd Mansion in North Berwick to Be Restored." January 10, 1968.

Yorke, Dane. *A History and Stories of Biddeford.* Biddeford, ME: Library Collection, McArthur Public Library, 1994.

ABOUT THE AUTHOR

Roxie J. Zwicker grew up in western Massachusetts and has always been intrigued by local history and ghost stories. One of the first stories she collected was about the haunted Victorian house beside her grammar school. Traveling down back roads and learning about the unique character and characters of New England is one of her favorite things to do. She is the owner of New England Curiosities, a tour and event company located in Portsmouth, New Hampshire. She started doing ghost tours in Carver, Massachusetts, in 1993 and has been doing tours along the seacoast since 2002. Roxie has been featured in national magazines and newspapers, from *Better Homes and Gardens* to *USA Today*. She has also filmed with New England Cable News, the Travel Channel and the History Channel.

Besides *Haunted York County*, she has also written *Haunted Cemeteries of New England*, *Haunted Portsmouth*, *Haunted Pubs of New England* and *Haunted Portland*.

Visit her website at www.newenglandcuriosities.com for more information.

Visit us at
www.historypress.net